RYCHARDE CURE DE LYON

EARLY TUDOR DRAMA

MEDWALL, THE RASTELLS, HEYWOOD, AND THE MORE CIRCLE

BY

A. W. REED, M.A., D.Lit.

UNIVERSITY READER IN ENGLISH LANGUAGE AND
LITERATURE, KING'S COLLEGE, LONDON

WITH NINE ILLUSTRATIONS

METHUEN & CO. LTD.
36 ESSEX STREET W.C.
LONDON

read a paper before the Bibliographical Society on
John Rastell, which I did on 19th November, 1917,
to an interesting audience presided over by the late
Sir William Osler, the paper appearing subsequently
in the *Transactions* of the society in 1920. Mean-
while, in July 1918, Mr. Pollard had printed in
The Library my article on the *Wydow Edyth*, and
I recall the difficulty of handling the proofs in a hut
as a full private. A short leave granted after the
Armistice enabled me unexpectedly to read myself,
on 18th November, 1918, before the Bibliographical
Society, the paper on " The Regulation of the Book
Trade before the Proclamation of 1538," which
appeared in due course in the *Transactions*. *The
Library* for January 1919 contained my article on
" John Rastell's Plays ", and when the paper had
been printed which I read on 19th February, 1923,
before the society on " William Rastell, the Editor
of More's English Works ", Mr. Pollard might have
claimed to have rounded off my work.

In the course of my talks with him I had told
him of a discovery I had made at the Museum of
the Caxton source of Henry Medwall's *Fulgens and
Lucres* and of information I had been able to
gather about this as well as about Medwall. Of
this remarkable play only the Bagford fragment of
two leaves was then known, and when Mr. Pollard
told me early in 1919 that the perfect Mostyn copy
was announced for sale by Sotheby's, I had the
exciting experience of handling the play in the
sale-room and of saying what I knew of Medwall,
his play, and its sources in an article in *The Times
Literary Supplement* on 3rd April, 1919.

The inquiries into the dating of John Heywood's

plays, upon which I had at first set out, had become much wider than I had expected; and when Sir Israel Gollancz, at whose suggestion I had begun my searches, invited me to read a paper before the Shakespeare Association on 29th February, 1920, I chose as my title, " The Beginnings of the English Secular and Romantic Drama," a title which seems to me to represent fairly accurately what my work has led me to. Since then I have had the pleasure of collaborating with my friend, Dr. F. S. Boas, in producing an edition of *Fulgens and Lucres* based on the facsimile published, with characteristic public spirit, by Mr. Henry Huntington, the American owner of the Mostyn copy.

I am justified, I think, in referring thus at some length to the history of my indebtedness to Mr. Pollard, and in retaliating upon him for the very generous references he has made to my work in his *English Miracle Plays*, by indicating how very much he himself is responsible for any little disturbance I may have caused in his earlier account of the *Interlude*.

But the papers and articles that I have been publishing in this way since 1917 are necessarily scattered and are not generally accessible, and I have had it in mind for some time to make them into a book. This I could do in one of two ways, either by rewriting the whole and so avoiding the repetitions and loose ends that seemed to be inevitable in a number of papers contributed at different times for different purposes, or by altering the original form of my work as little as possible and trusting to my ability so to rearrange it that it should exhibit its own continuity and unity. I

CONTENTS

xiii

LIST OF ILLUSTRATIONS

EARLY TUDOR DRAMA

CHAPTER I

JOHN RASTELL, PRINTER, LAWYER, VENTURER, DRAMATIST, AND CONTROVERSIALIST

I

THERE were two John Rastells, men of distinction in the reign of Henry VIII, the one a wealthy cloth-maker of Gloucester, whose antecedents are known to us from a Chancery suit,[1] and the other, the subject of this paper, John Rastell, the printer, brother-in-law of Sir Thomas More. The printer's family belonged to Coventry, where Thomas Rastell, presumably his grandfather, held office as Warden in 1443.[2] The Warden's son, Thomas Rastell, was a man of legal attainments. In 1471 he took an active part in meeting the troubles that fell upon Coventry after the defeat and death of Warwick at Barnet. Later he sat on the Commission for Warwickshire, and along with Sir Thomas Lyttelton, was one of the Quorum.[3] This association would be in his son's mind when he printed Lyttelton's *Tenures*.

The earliest notice of John Rastell occurs in the Corpus Christi Gild Book in 1489, when the first of a series of instalments of his gild fee was paid on his behalf by Joan Symonds, widow of an ex-mayor of Coventry. The entry of the second instalment mentions his father, Thomas. If his admission was at the age of fourteen, 1475 would be the year of his birth.

[1] P.R.O., Early Chancery Proceedings, 439/10.
[2] *Coventry Leet Book* (E.E.T.S.), ed. Dormer Harris.
[3] Pat. Rolls, Ed. IV 1478–80.

Rastell's legal education was probably acquired at the Middle Temple, for there is a reference in the Bench Book to a fine on " Rastell an utter Barrister for absence from the Parliament of the Inn ", dated 29th January, 1501–2.

An entry [1] in Henry VII's Book of Payments shows that he was already associated with the Mores in 1499 when John More, John Rastell, Thomas More, and another furnished securities for the repayment of a loan or debt of one hundred marks, an obligation which they duly met in the following year.

That he was already married by 1504 to Elizabeth More is suggested by a Hustings Deed at the Guildhall of that year (231/1–2) of a quit-claim of a tenement by Sir John More to his sons-in-law John Rastell and Richard Staverton. John More had been fined £100 by way of retaliation for the action of his son Thomas in successfully resisting in Parliament the royal demand for a subsidy of three-fifteenths. While his father thus set about raising the £100, Thomas More sought the seclusion of the Charterhouse, where he found peace of mind in the translation of the Life of Pico della Mirandula and consolation in penning Latin epigrams on tyrants.

Rastell's early married life was spent in Coventry, where, in 1506, he succeeded his father as Coroner, presiding over the Court of Statute Merchant, and acting as clerk of recognizances of debts. It was during this time that he was visited by his brother-in-law, and we have an entertaining account of an adventure that befell More during the visit. The story which is translated in the Preface to Day's *Descant on the Psalms*, is found in one of More's Latin letters defending Erasmus's *New Testament*, printed in the *Epistolae aliquot eruditorum* of 1520. More went to Coventry to see his sister and had no sooner alighted than the unexpected question was put to him whether a man could be eternally damned who daily read Our Lady's Psalter. It seems that an old Franciscan had established the cult of the Psalter

[1] P.R.O., King's Book of Payments, E. 415/31 (f. 20 r.).

in Coventry, and excited a remarkable public following; for, says More, " he showed so easy a way to Heaven ". But More was not allowed to find shelter in his sense of humour. He was asked out to supper and the Friar turned up with a boy, " a tergo cum codicibus ". The question was asked again. More kept silence, the Friar " barked and brawled " for two hours. Then More replied judicially that though a prince might grant a pardon at the queen's request he would hardly make a law granting immunity to all who should perform some office for her. But the Friar was mightily extolled, and More laughed at for a fool.

The circumstances referred to in More's anecdote are illustrated in an interesting way by the will of Thomas Bonde, who, like many of the cloth merchants of the Midlands, was a " merchant of the Staple of Calais ". He died early in 1507, during Rastell's Coronership, and founded by his will the well-known " bede-house " and Chapel at Bablake in Coventry for ten poor men of the two great Gilds of the Trinity and Corpus Christi, " the said x poore men (being) bounden euery day to say three times Our Lady's Psalter for all the brethren and sustren of the Trinity Guild . . . and at every dirige they shall set knelyng and say our ladyes psalter ".[1]

In the same year (1507) there died at Coventry a wealthy mercer, Richard Cooke,[2] like Bonde an ex-Mayor, who appointed Rastell an overseer of his will. After directing that " there shall be as little coste done at his burials as may be with honestie ", he bequeaths one *Bible in English* to Trinity Church, Coventry, and another to Walsall Parish Church. Here, on the other hand, we have an apparent case of Lollardry, and it is interesting to find that Rastell was looked upon as the kind of man who might be expected to see Cooke's directions carried out. One wonders if it led to Rastell's resignation of the Coronership in 1508–9. The *Bible in English* can only have been the English version associated with Wycliff's name and for

[1] P.C.C. 22, Adeane.   [2] *Ibid.* 29, Adeane.

to success in his long fight on behalf of the commoners and craftsmen against a conservative Recorder and the ruling classes. Discontent at the invasion of the public grazing rights on the Lammas lands and a general resentment under a sense of oppression, demanded only a resolute leader to move the poorer citizens to mutiny, and this leader they found in Saunders, who, it should be noted, was himself of the privileged classes, son of a former mayor of the city.[1]

Rastell emerged from these and like experiences a radical reformer, and there is little in the social criticism of his brother-in-law's *Utopia* with which he would not find himself in hearty agreement.

Moreover, just as the city was divided by social problems, so in religious life there was a well-established cleavage. The Prior and the conservative churchmen had long been opposed by the upholders of the right of the lay folk to control the public instruction of their children. The town had insisted on the maintenance of a schoolmaster who, being paid by one of their guilds, should be under citizen control. But this spirit of independence had untoward results, and Coventry had a sad record of Lollard burnings. Here again Rastell's subsequent history suggests that he was of the party of the Reformers, and the office he was called upon to execute as overseer of Cooke's will in 1507 shows that he was then one of those who urged the recognition of the *Bible in English*.

The wealthiest citizens of Coventry were merchants of the Staple of Calais. Rastell's associations with them, both socially and professionally, were intimate, and it is natural that he should be accustomed to look with wide interest on life beyond the narrow seas. It cannot be postulated that it was Coventry that bred in him the spirit of the venturer, but it is unlikely that a lawyer more than forty years old should attempt a voyage to the New Found Lands with a cargo of stuffs, unless the impulse of adventure, speculation and travel had been confirmed in him when he was younger.

[1] *Coventry Leet Book.*

II

The passage from life in Coventry to life in London
was probably not an abrupt one. Rastell was well known
in London legal circles as a member of the More family ;
but by 1512 he was in the service of Sir Edward Belknap,
brother-in-law of Henry Smyth of Coventry, Clerk of the
King's Works, and had moved south. A Privy Councillor
to Henry VII and Henry VIII, Belknap held many offices
of trust ; he was frequently employed on special work in
France, and important diplomatic negotiations were
entrusted to him.[1] Rastell served with him through the
French War of 1512–14.

Two documents belonging to the month of December
1514 throw light on the nature of Rastell's services in the
war. From these we learn that he was appointed by Belknap
overseer for the unloading at the Tower of " eighteen
hoyes lately comen from Calais with the kinges ordenance
and fare cartes ", and later for the " drawing (of) two great
gonnes called culyvers into the Bulwerk and bearing iron
shott into the Tower and bestowing cartes from the Tower
wharf dispatched oute of (certain other) hoies ". He is described as John Rastell, Gent. ; he had a subordinate officer
and a considerable body of carpenters and labourers under
him and was paid at the rate of twelve pence a day. The
transport of artillery, without which Henry could not have
taken Terouenne, was one of the chief problems of the
campaign. From the fact that Rastell was appointed to
see the guns and carriages safely " bestowed " when their
work was done, we may infer that he had won respect by
his achievements in similar undertakings. Hall's account
of the campaign and his references to the foundering of
heavy guns in soft ground suggest that Rastell may well
have found opportunities of showing his resourcefulness.

[1] The activities of Belknap are fully recorded in *Letters and Papers of
Henry VIII*. Dugdale deals with his Warwickshire associations. He is
not noticed in the *D.N.B.*

became confiscate to the Crown, and his daughters, Margaret and Mary, became the King's wards.

In January 1514–15 Rastell took a country house at Monken Hadley, near High Barnet, on a thirty years' lease at a rental of £6 3s. 4d., and on the 25th April following he acquired a ten years' lease of a manor hard by, named Lydgraves, which is described in Lyson's *Middlesex*. These leases, it will be noticed, were taken more than six months before he signed and could have benefited from the Hunne indenture.

Both the Hadley leases led to law-suits.[1] the one in Chancery in 1519, and the other a Court of Requests Case in 1532.[2] From the latter case we learn that Rastell had converted a tile house at Hadley into a " fair-hall ", " well-devised ", besides building a new house for a tenant. He made a parlour and chambers, with three or four bay windows well glased and three goodly chimneys. The grounds which were overgrown with shrubs and briars he converted into a " fayr meadow ". He " dicked and quike-set fourty poles of garden ", and " cast five ponds for fisshe ". Here, said Lowe, one of the witnesses, " he entertained Maistre Cromwell, Mr. Frowick and divers others at a shoting, rennyng and other games made by the said Rastell ", who told this witness that the " fair house was his own device ". It was indeed " a fair house to lodge in ", added Lowe, " and Maister Cromwell, Mr. Geoffrey Chambre and many other lay in the same house." Nevertheless, Rastell lost his suit, and his " fair house ", but the law-suit, of course, belongs to the close of his life. In 1514–15 we see him, then, establishing himself in a country house not far from Sir John More's Manor house of Gobions at North Mymmes, and this " fair hall " with its five fish ponds, forty poles of garden, its fair meadow, its goodly chimneys, its bay windows well glazed and its parlour and chambers, remained his for nearly twenty years, and when he lost it it was on condition that he received the

[1] E.C.P., 560/60.
[2] Court of Requests (1532) and Orders and Decrees Book 5, f. 212.

value of his " ameliorations ". By December 1516 the
three volumes of his *Grand Abridgment* were published,
but the same date witnessed the publication of a work much
better known to us, his brother-in-law's *Utopia*.

The adventures of Hythloday seem to have excited
Rastell, for six months later he was off in the *Barbara* of
Greenwich on no less a quest than a voyage of discovery
to the New Found Lands. On 5th March next ensuing,
the King's Letters of Recommendation [1] were granted to
John Rastell, and two other London citizens who purposed
to go on business of the King's and of their own " ad longin-
quas mundi partes ".

Ravyn, the purser of Rastell's ship, the *Barbara*, was a
well-known seaman, and so too was Richards, the master.
They were typical master mariners of the early Tudor navy.
Having got Rastell as far as Waterford with many delays,
and having no intention whatever of going any farther
west, they suggested to him that it would pay him better
to give up his voyage and " fall to robbing upon the sea ".
Faced with mutiny, and separated from the rest of the fleet,
Rastell landed at Waterford and appears to have tried to
find new officers ; whereupon Ravyn threatened to sail off
and sell the cargo at Bordeaux, which he ultimately did.
Rastell seems to have been altogether beaten by his mutinous
mariners, for, having forced him to give them an acquittance
of their undertaking, they left him in Ireland to find his own
way home. There is reason to believe that he remained
in Ireland for some considerable time, but on his return
he successfully prosecuted Ravyn ; and the whole story is
told with a remarkable wealth of detail in the depositions
of the witnesses called on Rastell's behalf.[2] Ravyn disputed
the decision later in a Chancery suit.

Since there were two feats that the Utopians had to
thank Hythloday and his companions for, " the scyence
of imprinting and the craft of making paper," it is not
surprising to find that Rastell took with him his servant

[1] Rymer XIII, 582, and French Rolls, 8.H.8.   [2] See Appendix XI.

" Thomas Bercula, printer ", on his voyage to the New Found Lands.

The account of Rastell's voyage in the Court of Requests case has a twofold interest ; it bears out the evidence of Bale that John Rastell was the author of the interlude *The Four Elements*, and it proves that an important voyage to the New Found Lands was organized in 1516–17 and failed. I have spoken only of Rastell's part in the undertaking, but the depositions show that there was a fleet, and that the mutiny was organized, probably with the approval of the Earl of Surrey, the Lord High Admiral. A passage in one of Sir Richard Eden's prefaces refers to this voyage as being organized under Sebastian Cabot and Sir Thomas Spert, through whose faint-heartedness, he says, it failed. This reference of Eden's which has been disputed, must now be allowed to stand.

We shall have occasion to deal with Rastell's interlude later, but in a long and spirited passage, highly imperialistic in tone, he displays his indignation :

> But they that were the venturers
> Have cause to curse their maryners
> Fals of promys and dissemblers
> That falsly them betrayed.

Rastell had probably sunk no small part of the Hunne fortune in this enterprise, and he appears to have been bound to find securities for advances made from the Royal Treasury ; for in the summer of the voyage John More and John Rastell had been bound in three obligations to pay 250 marks by 1521, and Rastell's friends, Geoffrey and Christopher Wren, for a like amount by 1520.

As a printer, Rastell is known to have put up his sign at three shops ; first, as we have already said, at the Abbot of Winchecombe's Place by the Fleet bridge in St. Bride's Parish ; next on the south side of St. Paul's ; and finally at Paul's Gate in Cheapside. It has been generally accepted, on the evidence of the Bridge House case discovered by

Mr. Plomer, that Rastell moved to Paul's Gate in 1520. If we calculate from the dates given by Rastell's own Bill, which is among the uncalendared Chancery Proceedings, we might make out a case for 1518, for speaking before 28th January, 1534–5, Rastell states that he had then paid rent for the Bridge House shop at Paul's Gate for over sixteen years. I have, however, been permitted to consult the " Bridge House Rentals " at the Guildhall, and find that Rastell paid rent at the annual rate of £5 6s. 8d. for his Mermaid premises at Paul's Gate from Michaelmas 1519 to 1536,[1] the last payment being made *post mortem*. But we have now to consider Rastell in a new light.

In the spring of 1520 there was entrusted to Sir Edward Belknap and Sir Nicholas Vaux the erection of the great Hall at Guisnes for the Field of the Cloth of Gold. Three thousand workmen, Arnold tells us, were occupied on the buildings for four months, and Rastell was called in specially for the making and garnishing of the roofs of the Banqueting Hall. In this part of the work he was associated with Richard Gibson, Sergeant of the Tents and Revels, Clement Urmston and John Brown, the King's painter. Twice in one week in the spring of that year Belknap and Vaux wrote to Wolsey urging him to send Rastell and the others across without delay " to make and garnish all the rofes, a marvellous great charge, for the rofes be large and stately ". They ask also that Alexander Barclay, the " Black Monk " and poet,[2] be sent " to devise histories and convenient raisons to flourish the buildings and banquet house withal ". In spite of Belknap's anxiety the work was finished, and in his rapturous description of the glories of the building, Hall, the Chronicler, fails to find words adequate to tell the splendours of the roofs, which, he says, " were covered with cloth of silke, *of the most faire and quicke invention* that before that time was seen . . . furnished so to mannes sight that no livyng creature might

---

[1] The importance of these dates for bibliographers is considerable. Books issued by Rastell from the south side of Paul's are earlier than 1519 ; those from Paul's Gate are later.

[2] The author of the *Eclogues* and translator of *The Ship of Fools*.

but joye in the beholding thereof ". Brewer, in the *Letters and Papers of Henry VIII*, rather lost the point, I think, when he read " roses " for " rofes ".

We now return to London to Paul's Gate. Here Rastell's shop by the archway into Paul's Churchyard faced the Church of St. Michael's in the Quern which stood in Cheapside where the Peel statue now stands. At the east end of St. Michael's was the " Littel Conduit in Cheap ", and we learn from the Town Clerk's Records [1] that Rastell was authorized to erect a pageant here " at the lytel Conduit " in the summer of 1522 at a cost not exceeding £15. This was in honour of the visit of the Emperor Charles V, who passed through the City to St. Paul's with Henry VIII. I shall have more to say of this pageant later.

Financial problems were now probably giving Rastell some anxiety. He and John More were bound to repay to the Crown 250 marks by 1521 in respect of the voyage, and at Michaelmas 1522, there were also due to the Crown from Rastell by the terms of the Hunne indentures the payment of 810 marks. He failed to meet the latter obligation, and his enemies seized the opportunity thus offered to them.

Soon after he had entered into Hunne's estate, Rastell made an agreement with one of his sureties, Geoffrey Wren, a Royal Chaplain, to divide equally with him the " bargayn " and its responsibilities, and from that mortgage arose Rastell's troubles. For a certain Wm. Whaplode successfully importuned Wren to persuade Rastell to give Margaret Hunne in marriage to his son, Roger Whaplode, and bonds were entered into for the due payment of a certain sum as dowry [2] in quittance of all claims. Rastell asserts that the Whaplodes neither legally concluded nor carried out these bonds, and in 1523, going behind them, they succeeded in a petition to the King for the forfeiture of Rastell's original

[1] Repertories, 5/284.
[2] It had been Rastell's original intention to marry the Hunne girls to his own two sons, thereby keeping the dowries in the family.

securities and of all Hunne's papers and effects. This course was rendered possible by Rastell's failure to fulfil his obligation to the Crown of paying 810 marks due in 1522. Letters Patent were granted to the Whaplodes on the 4th May, 1523, restoring to them all Hunne's lands and tenements and all leases and deeds relating thereto ; also the indenture between John Rastell and the King of 7th October, 1515, and all the goods, chattels, and debts specified therein ; also the King's right and interest in the five separate obligatory deeds by which Rastell and others were bound in various sums.

I look upon this reverse to Rastell as a fact capable of an explanation. Hunne's case had excited great attention in the City. His heresy was forgotten in the admiration felt for one who had endured martyrdom rather than pay a *mortuary*.

The City was fighting the " Curates " and their tithes and offerings. But the year 1523 was the year of the great Subsidy, the success of which depended not a little on Wolsey's ability to win the sympathy of the City, and it may be that this concession to the Whaplodes was a politic act. It must also be remembered that Rastell's old patron, Belknap, had died suddenly in 1521, and that it was to Belknap that Rastell owed the Hunne grant.

The Whaplodes at once attacked Rastell and his sureties at Common Law, and Rastell sought refuge in a Chancery suit. In 1526 the case went to arbitration before the Lord Chief Justice, Sir Anthony Fitzherbert, and Sir Lewis Pollard,[1] and the Whaplodes were awarded 400 marks. Rastell immediately paid down £100, but before the award could be duly drawn and sealed, one of the arbitrators, Sir Lewis Pollard, died, and the Whaplodes again attacked Rastell at Common Law ; but they almost certainly had to accept the award mentioned, for I find from Foxe, to whom, of course, Hunne was a hero, that the Whaplodes were keeping alive the feeling of animosity in the City against Rastell

[1] E.C.P., 560/51.

by other means in 1529 ; for in that year Roger Whaplode
had the following Bill read by a preacher at the Spital :

A Bill Read by the Preacher at the Spital.

" If there be any well disposed person willing to do any cost
upon the reparation of the conduit in Fleet Street, let him or
them resort unto *the Administrators of the goods and cattle of
one Richard Hunne*, late merchant tailor of London which died
intestate, or else to me, and they shall have toward the same
six pounds thirteen shillings and four pence, and a better penny,
of the goods of the said Richard Hunne ; upon whose soul, and
all christian souls Jesus have mercy ! "

In other words Rastell was still in possession of the Hunne
estate in 1529. " For the Bill ", Foxe says, " Whaplode was
brought and troubled before the Bishop ", the preacher was
suspended from saying Mass, and had to read a recantation
at Paul's Cross acknowledging the offence of praying for the
soul of one adjudged a heretic by the laws of Holy Church !

In the end Rastell was successful,[1] and if our reading
of the evidence is right, Wolsey made some amends as
Chancellor for the wrong he did Rastell in 1525. Instead
of 810 marks to the Crown, Rastell paid 400 marks to the
Whaplodes and apparently kept his use of the estate in
spite of the Letters Patent granted to his opponents. " As
a man is friended so the law is ended ". John Rastell was
probably as difficult a defendant to outpoint as one might
expect to meet.

On Michaelmas Day, 1524, while the Hunne case was
running its course, Rastell took from the Prioress of Holywell
a forty years' lease [2] of an acre and three roods of ground
having a frontage on Old Street, and lying in Finsbury
Fields. Here be built himself a house and laid out grounds,
and it was here that he built the stage to which reference
is made in the Court of Requests case [3] published by
Mr. Plomer and reprinted by Mr. A. W. Pollard in *An English*

---

[1] A later appeal to Cromwell by the Whaplodes shows this.
[2] R.O. Conventual Leases (Middlesex), No. 30, and Appendix V.
[3] R.O., Court of Requests, 8/14.

Garner : Fifteenth Century Prose and Verse. As this is the earliest stage known to the historian of the Tudor drama, its position in the district that Burbage and Alleyn made famous in Elizabeth's reign is not without interest. Rastell's Finsbury property is now, I believe, covered by the head offices of Bovril, Limited.

Whilst he was occupied with his new property at Finsbury, Rastell published two small books whose nature suggests that his litigious troubles were not seriously worrying him. The first was *The XII Merry Jests of the Wydow Edyth,* an entertaining work in Chaucerian verse by Walter Smyth, personal servant of Sir Thomas More, and later Sword Bearer to the Lord Mayor. The other was the first of the Tudor jest books, the famous *Hundred Merry Tales,* a compilation in which Rastell himself had a hand. To the period 1526-9 we must assign the plays printed by Rastell, *Gentleness and Nobility,* of which he himself was the author, and *Calisto and Meliboea* which shows almost unmistakable marks of his workmanship.[1]

There is interest for bibliographers in a record of Rastell's relations with a young printer, Laurence Andrewe, at this time. It occurs in a Chancery suit [2] heard by Wolsey, probably in 1527-8, and shows that Andrewe had borrowed £5 and £20 worth of printing material from Rastell. Andrewe fled abroad leaving Rastell to prosecute his aunt, Mistress Andrewe, the Prioress of Stamford, who seems to have acted as a sponsor for the borrower.

In the summer of 1527, Ambassadors came from France to arrange a marriage with Princess Mary, the daughter of Henry and Catherine, and were most splendidly entertained at Greenwich. Hans Holbein prepared a wonderful representation of the " Taking of Terouenne " and Rastell devised a pageant called the " Father of Heaven ". Hall's description, supplemented by that of the Venetian, Spinelli, gives a detailed account of the pageant and its setting, but

---

[1] See Chapter III.
[2] Chancery Proceedings, 564/27. See appendix.

C

we have also valuable evidence in the accounts of Rastell's expenses kept by Sir Henry Guildford, the Treasurer.[1]

It appears from these accounts that Walton, the builder of Rastell's Finsbury stage, was employed by Rastell as a stage carpenter in the preparations for 26 days at 8d. a day. " Maister Mann ", the King's painter, received 12d. for making the pictures and 9d. a day for 27 days, and ten workmen were engaged for about 3 weeks at 6d. a day. The most interesting personal item, however, is that Rastell's son, William, now 19 years old, was employed on the preparations by his father for 44 days at 8d. a day.

There were two halls built for the festivities, one for the banquet, the other, with seats arranged in tiers along either side, for the pageantry. After the feast, the guests were marshalled to see the Holbein picture which was shown on the other side of the great arch through which they passed to take their places in the second hall. " The rofe of thys chambre was cunnyngly made ", says Hall, " by the King's Astronomer ", but Guildford's accounts show it to be Rastell's work. " On the ground of the rofe was made the hole earth environed with the sea, like a very Mappe or Carte, and by a conning makyng of a nother cloth, the zodiacke with the XII signes, and the five circles or girdelles and the two poles apered on the earth, and water compassing the same, and in the zodiak were the twelve signes, curiously made, and above this were made the seven planets as Mars, Jupiter, Sol, Mercurius, Venus, Saturne and Luna, every one in their proper houses, made according to their properties, that it was a cunnyng thing and a pleasant syght to beholde."

Two-thirds down the hall, under an arch all gilt, the King took his seat, and at his feet the two queens. There then entered on either side singers who sang English songs, and in the centre a handsome young man advanced clad in sky blue silk spangled with eyes, representing Mercury. After delivering to the King a greeting from Jupiter, the

[1] R.O., Misc. Bks., Excheq. T.R., 227, p.

" Father of Heaven ", Mercury announced that, having
often heard disputed the question of the relative merits of
Love and Riches, Jove now refers the decision to the King,
whereupon, Mercury retiring, there follows an Interlude in
the form of a *débat* between a chorister Cupid and his
decani supporters, and Plutus with his *cantoris* followers.
This debate is fully described by Hall and Spinelli.

For the writing [1] of the Dialogue, that is, of course, the
Interlude of *Love and Riches*, and for Mercury's Latin address
to the King, Rastell charged the modest fee of 3s. 4d.
In all, his account came to £26 11s. 3d. There is no item
showing his own fee, which would no doubt appear in the
King's Book of Payments ; but that, unfortunately, is
missing for this period.

It will be convenient at this point to say something further
of Rastell's pageants. It will be remembered that he devised
a pageant at the Lyttyl Conduit by Paul's Gate in 1522,
when Charles V and the King went to St. Paul's. Here,
according to Hall, " there was builded a place like heaven,
curiously painted with clouds, orbes, starres and hierarchies
of angels. In the top of the pageant was a great type, and
out of the type sodainly issued out of a cloud a fayre lady
richely apparelled, and then all the minstrels which were in
the pageant played and the angel sang, and sodainly again
she was assumpted into the cloud, which was very curiously
done, and aboute this pageant stode the apostles " whereof
one said Latin verses which Hall then gives. [2]

Here, as at Greenwich, the astronomical character of the
device is emphasized, the heaven, clouds, orbs and stars ;
whilst the hierarchies of angels suggest that Rastell may
have devised the pageant of the " Nine Hierarchies of
Angels " at Coventry in 1510, when the King and Queen
visited the City. When we remember that it was upon the
roofs that he worked for the Field of the Cloth of Gold,
we may perhaps assume that they, too, were astronomical
in character. Rastell's well-known printer's device, showing

[1] I.e., the scribe's work.   [2] Another account is given later.

the Father of Heaven, the Merman and Mermaid, the heavenly bodies, and under all the Four Elements, preserves, not unfitly, the note of cosmography and of pageantry that Rastell had made his own. Finally, as bearing on Rastell's interest in astronomy, I would point out that his contemporary, Bale, after referring to his pre-eminence in mathematics, "demonstrable science", and cosmography, mentions a work that is either unidentified or lost, his *Canones Astrologici*.

The fact that his son William was working with his father at Greenwich in 1527 warrants us, I think, in assuming that he took part also in the increased activity of Rastell's press between 1526 and 1530, when, setting up his own press, at the age of twenty-one, he issued his first book.

During these years, assisted by his son, Rastell printed several law books, including an *Abbreviation of the Statutes*, with an interesting preface ; he published More's *Dialogue of Images*, his own *Book of Purgatory*, and his remarkable chronicle with the punning title, *The Pastyme of People*. Rastell's printing therefore appears to fall into two well-marked periods, the Fitzherbert period from about 1512 to 1518 and the later period from 1526 to 1530, when he had his son William with him. To this later period should be assigned the undated plays, *Gentleness and Nobility* and *Callisto*. It is interesting to note that William Rastell afterwards printed an edition of Fabyan's *Chronicle*, the source of the greater part of *The Pastyme of People*.

Meanwhile, at this period, Rastell was unusually busy at Westminster Hall, and particularly so during the time of More's Chancellorship from 1529 to 1532. A reform in Chancery proceedings, attributed to More, but actually due to Wolsey, enables us to estimate Rastell's activity as a Chancery lawyer. To reduce the number of frivolous Bills of Complaint, Wolsey had all Chancery Bills examined and signed by lawyers of standing. During Wolsey's Chancellorship Rastell's signature appears on his own Bills, but I have not come across it on others. Under More

PRINTER'S DEVICES USED BY JOHN RASTELL
FROM THE BRITISH MUSEUM COPY OF RASTELL'S 'LIBER ASSISARUM' (1513)

his signature is frequent. We may note, however, that whilst he was well known as a plaintiff before the Chancellors Warham, Wolsey, and Audeley, he never appeared as plaintiff before More.

In 1530 Sir John More died, and his death led, I think, to some weakening of the family tie between Rastell and the Mores. This weakening of the family tie gradually became an actual breach, and when More was put to death in 1535, Rastell was very definitely in the camp of his opponents.

We have reached the last chapter of his life, a chapter to be understood only if we recognize as the central fact that he now attached himself whole-heartedly, and with tragic consequences, to the service of Thomas Cromwell.

In 1529 he became a member for a Cornish borough in the Reformation Parliament that served so effectively the purposes of Cromwell and the King; and in 1529–30, he spent six months in France, engaged, it may be, in seeking academic support for the divorce. In the new *Book of Purgatory*, published in 1530, he provoked to controversy More's opponent, the young Protestant, John Frith, and supported the old doctrine with all his old ardour, by "natural reason and good philosophy". Bale says that Frith's reply converted the older man to the reformed faith, and the fact that Frith was capable of conducting a debate in excellent good humour, while his life was in jeopardy, makes the statement plausible. An instance of Frith's sense of fun may be of interest.

Rastell was apparently given to writing nonsense verses taking here and there incongruous lines from different ballads. There is a good example in his play of the *Four Elements* :

> Robyn hode in barnysdale stode
> And lent hym tyl a mapyll thystyll
> Thar cam our lady and swete Saynt Andrewe
> Slepyst thou wakyst thou geffrey coke, etc.

He tried the following lines on Frith :

> In the beginning of this year
> John Frith is a noble clerk
> He killed a millstone with his spear
> Keep well your geese, the dogs do bark.

But Frith rejoined, " as touching the metre, the second verse lacketh a foot and is shorter than his fellows ", and he made the following emendation :

> In the beginning of this year
> John Rastell is a noble clerk, etc.

If all who were writing English verse in 1530 had shown Frith's regard for iambics, Tottell's *Miscellany* would have had less significance in the history of English prosody.

III

We must now picture Rastell to ourselves as the energetic, ingenious and devoted agent of Cromwell, engaged in the service of the Commonweal. The facts that I now have to put before the reader will show what use Cromwell made of him, and what, if anything, he did for his servant.

In Cromwell's *Remembrances* for 1532, among the Bills awaiting Royal signature is one for Rastell to be made Governor and Master of Christ Church, or the Priory of Holy Trinity, Aldgate. The plan seems to have been to secularize the establishment and make Rastell its first head. The scheme fell through and the property went to More's successor, Audeley.[1] Another draft Bill appears for the appointment of Rastell and another lawyer to a new office for the drawing up and sealing of legal instruments in the City, whereby the issue of fraudulent deeds might be checked. Possibly something came of this, as Rastell and his colleague were said to owe in 1534 £20 in " obli-

[1] Audeley was somewhat of an invalid and so, says Fuller, " he was allowed to carve for himself the first cut " from the monastic spoils. The priory was only surrendered because it was so deep in debt.

gacions ". In 1534 a letter from a John Arundel to Rastell " dwelling in Paternoster Row " casts a reflection upon Rastell's relations with Cromwell. Arundel promises £20 to Cromwell, and he hints at an equivalent reward for Rastell for Cromwell's good offices with the Bishop of Exeter in the matter of a lease, a Naboth's vineyard. This was the Arundel who, says Hall, " took Duncan Camall, a rover of Scotland, after a long fight ". The fact that this letter is among the Public Records shows that it reached Cromwell. Meanwhile, in 1533, the Surveyor of Crown Lands had granted a lease to Cromwell, Rastell and others, of all mining rights on Dartmoor.

In 1534 Rastell lost, as we have already seen, his law-suit against the Skipwiths and with it his fair house at Hadley, where he had lived for nineteen years. In the same year he was engaged with Roland Lee, Bishop of Coventry and Lichfield, on his mission for the checking of lawlessness in Wales. He carried reports to Cromwell from Lee, who in one letter asks for Cromwell's offices in Rastell's behalf. He describes him as " the pore man ", a " very gentleman ", one who " does not interrupt in his own behalf ". Clearly Rastell's services to the Commonweal were not enriching him, and this reflection is confirmed by the fact that in July 1534 he had completed the alienation of his family lands and properties in Warwickshire, and thus made final the severance of the Rastells and Coventry.

In the summer of 1533 he had taken as his sub-tenant at Paul's Gate a stationer, John Gough, who in 1528 had been imprisoned on suspicion of aiding in the sale of heretical books, and we learn from the Town Depositions [1] in the suit Rastell v. Sutton, Draper and the Bridge House Masters, summarized by Mr. Plomer, that " the servants of Rastell had printed dyvers books in the seyd prynting house syth the seid Gough hath been in the seid house."

Rastell had at this time a considerable printing scheme before him, which he describes in a series of three letters

[1] Chancery Proceedings, Town Depositions, Bundle 1.

to Cromwell, and in an important unsigned paper of notes in his own handwriting. These were written after Cromwell had been appointed Secretary, 17th April, 1534. He had drawn up, at great pains, a book which he called the *Book of the Charge*. This he sent to Cromwell, who submitted it to competent authorities and returned it to Rastell for revision. The *Book of the Charge*, printed and issued as from the King, was to be sent to all Judges and Stewards of Courts and Sessions, and by them publicly read " whereby not only the lernyd men themselves but also the people shall be instructed in true learning and brought from ignorance to knowledge of the true faith and to have no confidence in the pope nor his laws ". He tells Cromwell how much pains he has taken in " this and like matters ", for which he has had " nought but great loss and hinderaunce and hatred and disdain " ; " and if some which ye call priests and spiritual men knew it came of me, they for disdain would do what they could to hinder it ". He suggests that 10,000 to 20,000 of the *Book of the Charge* should be printed and " sparklyd abroad " among the people, at a cost of less than £100. For four or five years he has been compiling divers books opposing the pope's authority and he has ruined his business. Where he used to make £40 a year at Westminster Hall now he makes less than £10. From 200 or 300 reams of paper a year, his printing has fallen to 50 reams. His printing used to bring him in more than his pleading. Other men in Cromwell's service make more of themselves, but none have served him more loyally than he. " Syr," he says, " I am an old man, I loke not to lyf long, and I regard ryches as much as I do chyppes save only to have a lyffyng to lyff out of det. And I care as mych for worldly hono[r] as I care for the flying of a fether in the wind."

He adds the interesting information that he has " devised certain prayers to be put in primers of divers sorts ", some of which are printed already in a " lytyl primer which I did send unto the Court ". He asks for the privilege of printing this primer on an extensive scale. Possibly the primer known as Gough's *Primer* [1] of 1536 may be the one Rastell alludes to.

Later he suggests to Cromwell that seven Masters in Chancery should be appointed to aid the Lord Chancellor in dealing with cases of heresy and, further, that learned men be appointed to draw sermons in English which should be printed and sent to every curate with a command to preach or read them on Sundays.[2] He follows up these suggestions with " notes of works to be printed before Parliament meets ".

(1) A little book proving that priests may marry and work for their living. (2) A little book proving that men may not honour images nor offer unto them. (3) Another proving that the prayers of men that be here living for the souls of them that be dead can in no wise be profitable to them that be dead.

After that there follow " Bylles to be drawen against the next Parliament ".

(1) For priests marrying. (2) Against offering to images. (3) For the Reformation of the Common Law. (4) For the Reformation of the Court of Chancery. (5) Against excessive fees taken by law clerks.

In the summer of 1535 John Whalley, Cromwell's agent at the Charterhouse, wrote to his master reporting that Rastell had made a search among the books there and " removed the Statutes of Bruno and such like books ". He wrote again about the same time reporting that Rastell had been coming daily to the Charterhouse in Cromwell's name " to common with the monks and reconcile them if he may ". " Syr," says Whalley, " altho Mr. Rastell be a very properly learned and an honest man, and of good experience, yet I think he is not the man that shall prevail

---

[1] A copy bearing the royal arms is in the University Library, Cambridge : *Imprynted by Johan Gowhe dwellynge in London in Chepsyd next Paulys gate,* 1536.

[2] See reference to Clement Urmeston's *Book of Sermons,* on p. 26.

amongst them, for they laugh and jest at all things that he speaketh."

Rastell's suspicion of the attitude of " some whom ye call priestes and spiritual men " was well founded, for soon after this he was imprisoned for his opposition to the Royal Proclamation of 1535, which settled the old City dispute of tithes and offerings that Hunne had taken his part in twenty years earlier.

The facts are sufficiently clear, for it appears from a Theological Tract at the Record Office (ix. 19) that Rastell, examined by the Archbishop and his Court, denied that curates might claim their living by tithes and oblations, and he based his contention in characteristic fashion on the laws of nature, of man and of God, that he had expounded in the Preface to the *Book of the Assizes* in 1514. After the Bishop of Winchester had argued with him, Rastell " sung again his old song ", which wearied Cranmer, who said that if he had anything new to say he should be heard.

Other evidences show that he was treated as belonging to a set of over-zealous reformers among whom were Bale and Marshall, whose name has been preserved in Marshall's *Primer*.

But even Rastell's old friend Clement Urmston, who had worked with him at the Field of the Cloth of Gold and at the Greenwich festivities of 1527, passed his last years in the same strange ferment of opposition. There exists, in Urmston's handwriting at the Record Office, a long and violent tract on the tithes question as well as a MS. book of sermons of 363 pages.

On the 20th April, 1536, Rastell made his will, appointing the King and Ralph Cressey his executors. His executor reported his death on 25th June, 1536. He appears to have died in confinement, for his last letter is addressed from prison to Cromwell, as Lord Keeper of the King's Privy Seal, an office for which Cromwell's Patent is dated 8th July, 1536.

In this letter he speaks of himself as " now by long imprisonment brought to extreme misery, forsaken of his kinsmen, destitute of his friends, comfortless and succourless ", " the scorn of men and the outcast of the people ". " If I durst be bold to say it," he continues, " methinks I have great wrong this long season to have been kept in durance without coming to my answer."

To serve the Commonweal had been the goal of his ambition. It was the theme of his first *Preface* and his motive in printing the *Grand Abridgment*. For this he planned his voyage, and now at length under Cromwell time seemed to have brought him the great occasion. But there was a virtue that it was too late in life for Rastell to acquire. He had never been either cautious or discreet, and caution at least was necessary in the service of Henry VIII.

He is not one of the great figures of his time, yet there are few that illustrate more completely the eager restlessness, the varied interests and tragic ironies of the sixteenth century.

In 1536, the year of his father's death, John Rastell the younger, now a Gentleman of one of the Inns of Court, sailed with Master Hore and other Gentlemen, and they reached Labrador. Here they were so beset with hunger that they were reduced to watching an osprey's nest for the fish she brought her young. They ate raw herbs and roots. A seaman killed his mate while he stooped to take up a root, cut out pieces of his flesh and broiled them on the coals and greedily devoured him. Others joined him, and the company decreased in this way until the officers discovered the ghastly truth, and the captain made a notable oration " vouching the Scriptures from first to last what God had done in cases of distress for them that called upon Him ".

And such was the mercy of God, that the same night there arrived a French ship in that port well furnished with victuals, and such was the policie of the English that they became masters of the same, and changing ships and vittailing them, they set sail to come to England.

The French got back too, and complained to Henry VIII, who being moved by pity paid them from his own purse. I have closed my chapter with this story from Hakluyt, because it seems to me to speak for itself and make further comment on the old adventurer unnecessary.

CHAPTER II

THE HEYWOODS

I

IN dealing with Rastell we have been breaking new ground. His son-in-law, John Heywood, on the other hand, has attracted the notice of many generations of students, and has secured a place in our literary history. We have all heard of the sallies and rejoinders of " merry John Heywood ", of " the mad merry wit " who " made many mad plays ". These were the theme of Peacham, of Fuller, and the learned Camden ; Ben Jonson talked of them to Drummond. There is no doubt that Heywood was a man of mark in the social life of his time, famous for his singing, as a player on the virginals, as a wit, epigrammatist, dramatist, and even, according to Bale, as a dancer. His social standing was that of *generosus*, or gentleman. The engraving in the *Spider and the Flie* shows him to have been a tall, striking figure and represents him in an academic gown, with a short sword or dagger—a man with an eye to appearances. He was lord of the manor of Brokehall, in Essex, and owner of lands in Hertfordshire and Kent, not by royal gift, but purchase. He was measurer of linen cloths in the City of London and a member of the Mercer's Company. He had intimate friends in the Inns of Court, and from the age of twenty-two he was attached to the royal household. The object of the present chapter is to show him not only as an independent figure, but also as a member of the family circle with which we are dealing.

It is probable that his father was a man of legal training, a William Heywood, who was acting temporarily as coroner of Coventry in 1505–6, when his name occurs in the Corpus

Christi Gild book as " de Couentry corinr ". Thomas Rastell
was succeeded as coroner in 1506 by his son John, and my
reading of this evidence is that, associated with the Rastells
at Coventry in a legal office, we have a William Heywood,
whose son John, the subject of this study, married Joan
Rastell. It would seem that on Thomas Rastell's death,
William Heywood filled his office until John Rastell
was duly elected in his father's stead. As late as 1527
there was a Heywood practising as an attorney at Westminster Hall (Dogget Rolls, Index 5). An earlier association
of the names Heywood and Rastell occurs in the Coventry
records, when an Edward Heywood was admitted along
with John Rastell as a member of the Gild, and there are
other evidences in the Gild Book of a connection of the
Heywoods with Coventry ; but we may leave the question
of the Heywood parentage and pass on to deal with the
Heywood brothers.

John Heywood had three brothers : William, a prosperous
yeoman of the village of Stock, in Essex ; Richard, who bore
arms and was a partner of William Roper, as Prothonotary
of the King's Bench ; and " Sir Thomas the Parson ", a monk
of St. Osyth's in Essex, who was executed for saying Mass
in 1574.

William of Stock Harvard, in the Hundred of Chelmsford,
was the eldest brother.[1] Stock is five miles south-west of
Chelmsford. It is a picturesque and prosperous village on
the high ground south of the old Roman road to Colchester
and midway between Ingatestone and Billericay.

From the Parish Registers I find that William died in
1568. His name appears on a Subsidy Roll of Stock in 1542-3
and again in 1544, when his lands were assessed at £10.
In Bonner's Visitation of 1554 he is mentioned after the
churchwardens as a juror, but in the Protestant Grindal's
Visitation of 1561 he is not named. His will is among the

---

[1] This is made clear in Richard Heywood's will from the place assigned
to his brother William's male heirs in the entailing of the Manor of
Woolwich.

Commissary of London Wills (Essex and Herts), and there he describes himself as " yoman ". His property was copyhold and consisted of three crofts called Warrens, of 6 acres, a house called Slowhouse with 14 acres, and another holding of 16 acres. He left his kine to his wife " to give or sell dischargynge the hereatts ", the ancient tribute due to the Lord of the Manor on the death of a tenant. The local character of the will is important. The copyhold lands are in the parishes of Stock and Butsbury, and the names of overseers and witnesses are local, several of them occurring in a Court Roll (R.O., 172/24) as of the homage of the Manor of " Inge Gynge Joyberd Laundry, Hertford Stock in the parish of Buttysbury ".[1] This extraordinary manorial description is important because it explains a line in John Heywood's play of *Wether* otherwise unintelligible.

Readers of *Wether* will remember that Merry Report, the Vice of the play, a kind of Puck, had been sent by Jupiter to summon any mortals who had suggestions to offer for a general reform of the weather. He tells on his return where he has been, and closes his list of places with the strange line :

Ynge gyngiang Jayberd Paryshe of Butsbery.

As the play was printed in 1533, one may assume that William Heywood was already at Stock then, and that the fact was known to some of his brother's audience.[2]

[1] His " Cosyn Lyndsell " was appointed overseer of the will. Richard Lyndsell, father of William Heywood's overseer, was Butler of Lincoln's Inn and an associate of Sir John More.

[2] A William Heywood, Yeoman of the Crown, who was present at the funeral of Henry VII (R.O., L.C. 2, 1. f. 124), was pensioned at 6d. a day in 1516, and was still being paid in 1525 (L. & P.). He appears to have been associated with Devon and Cornwall particularly (L. & P., i. 550), and was probably not a member of the family.

There was a younger William Heywood, a Yeoman Usher who was pensioned at £6 a year at the time of the Eltham Reforms of the Household in 1525, and in a Subsidy Roll of the assessment of the Royal Household in 1542–3 was charged 11s. on his pension of £6 (Subsidy Roll 69/37, R.O.). Possibly this was the yeoman of Stock.

Wm. Rastell left in 1565 to John Heywood's daughter, Elizabeth Marvin,

It is interesting that there are Heywoods still in Stock, and probably there has been a continuous association with the district. For instance, William, the most prosperous of the yeoman's sons, died in 1607 at Crondon in Orsett Hamlet, less than a mile from Stock, and in 1850 there died at Orsett Hamlet, William Arthur Heywood, in whose memory there is a window in the church of Stock.

The dramatist's second brother, Richard, born in 1509, was twelve years his junior. His will was proved in 1570 (P.C.C., 18, Lyon). In it he makes bequests to "my brother Sir Thomas Heywood, the parson ", " to my brother John Heywood ", " to my cosyne Donne and his wife ", " to my cosyne Marwyne theire sister ", and " to my sister Heywood, late wife of William Heywood of Stoke in the countie of Essex ".

Richard Heywood was a wealthy man, and his friends were men of high standing in the legal world. He left a black gown and a ring to the Master of the Rolls, and his executors were Justice Southcote and Sergeant Manwood. Shortly before his death he bought for £1,200 three manors in Sussex. In 1555 he bought the manor of Woolwich, and he owned other properties in Kent. In Lincolnshire he owned Crown lands, including three manors and other properties. He had property in Middlesex and he owned a house in Salisbury

a ring inscribed W. H. (i. 3). I suggest that this W. H. was the lawyer, her grandfather. But the initials W. H. seem destined to raise literary problems.

It is worthy of note that William Cawthorne Unwin, Mary Unwin's son and Cowper's friend, was Rector of the parish of Stock from 1769 to his death in 1787. An amusing poem by Cowper, under the title of " The Yearly Distress, or Tithing Time at Stock in Essex," commemorates " The troubles of the worthy priest " :

> " For then the farmers come, jog, jog,
> Along the miry road,
> Each heart as heavy as a log
> To make their payments good.

> " One talks of mildew and of frost
> And one of storms of hail,
> And one of pigs that he has lost
> By maggots at the tail."

Court as well as the house in St. Bride's parish in which he dwelt.

He had entered Lincoln's Inn in 1534, and two years later was allowed to have a clerk to board " at the clerkes commons commonly called the verlettes commons ". In 1567 he and his colleague, Wm. Roper, were granted the two east chambers in the middle rooms in the " new buildings ", which still stand near the old gateway in Chancery Lane.[1] From this it appears that Roper and Heywood had their offices, as Prothonotaries of the King's Bench, in Lincoln's Inn. When Sir Roger Cholmeley founded Highgate School in 1562 he chose Richard Heywood as one of the six original governors (R.O., Pat. Rolls, 7 Eliz., Pt. 2), and he is described on the enrolment as Richard Heywood, of London, Armiger. His arms are given in Glover's Ordinary (Cott. Lib., D. 10, f. 410). His funeral was marshalled by the College of Arms and a crest of a " tiger's head transfixed by a shaft " was granted *de novo* for the obsequies.

The contrast between his circumstances and manner of life and those of his yeoman brother needs no emphasis. But though his will has no homely reference like his brother's to " the white mare " or " grey gelding ", he was interested in agriculture. He had a 100-acre pasture at Titney in Lincolnshire that suggests an enclosure and a sheep-run after the new manner. Indeed, we have proof that he had speculated in sheep. A Special Commission (R.O., No. 1353) was appointed to report as to payment of rent for common of pasture for 516 sheep in Lincolnshire by Richard Heywood, deceased. Whatever the contrast between their fortunes, it is clear from his will that Richard Heywood was in close touch with his brothers and relatives. He remembers the widows, his sister-in-law of Stock, and his niece, Elizabeth Marvin, John Heywood's daughter, who lived with the Donnes. There can be no doubt that his house would admit John Heywood to considerable intimacy

[1] Black Books of Lincoln's Inn.

D

with legal men, and we may assume that the technicalities
of law and the society of lawyers were amongst the things
with which John Heywood's relationship to the Mores,
Ropers and Rastells had made him quite familiar, and in
which he was probably interested. In any case we have
here an explanation of the fact that the first twenty-eight
chapters of Heywood's allegory, *The Spider and the Flie*,
consist for the most part of a close legal disputation, in the
course of which the Flie claims to be heard in Westminster
Hall rather than in the Spider's Lordship,[1] for, says the Flie:

> In Westminster Hall I am not forsaken
> But may be a termer all tymes and howrs
> And that in aparence passeth your powrs
> For as common report maie be a proofe
> There never comth copweb in that hall roofe.
>   (Cap. 14.)

The third of John Heywood's brothers, Sir Thomas the
Parson, was a monk of Chick or St. Osyth's, a monastery
of Austin Canons, situated on a creek of the Colne opposite
Brightlingsea, " a house kepyng grat hospitalyte for the
relief of dyvers smal townes about it ; and the steple also
ys a comon marke for maryners upon the seas " (Dr. Cox,
Essex, p. 250). The remains of an Austin Priory of Thoby
still exists near Stock.

In the " Acknowledgments of Supremacy ", 1534, John
Whederyke, *alias* Colchester, signed as abbot, and Thomas
Heywood's name was seventeenth on a list of twenty-one.
At the dissolution (1539) the abbot and monks were pen-
sioned, Thomas Heywood's pension being £6 13s. 4d.

The valuation of St. Osyth's and the inventory of possessions are unusually full (L. & P., XIV, i, No. 1326), and
attached to the bundle (R.O., Church Goods 10/26) is an
autograph letter from Abbot Whederyke to John Heywood
written on 9th May, 1540. The letter is an acknowledgment
of the due receipt of rent from John Heywood for the Manor

---

[1] An ecclesiastical court. See pp. 34 and 209–10 .

of Brookhall, of which he held a lease from the monastery, for £8 a year, and it is endorsed :

To my lovyng herty frende John Heywode, gentylman delyver thys speedely.

Cromwell seized into his own hands the abbey lands, but on his death in the following year the lease was restored under a grant dated 3rd December, 1540 :

" Dilecto servienti nostro John Heywood " of our manor of Brookhall recently in the possession of Thomas Cromwell lately attainted of high treason . . . for 21 years at a rent of £14 1. 6. and 12d increment.[1]

In the description of Richard Heywood's Arms in the Moseley Collection (Add. MS. 35333) there occurs the note, " ye 14th of June 1574 a fryar who was akin was executed ", and Holinshed says that Thomas Heywood was arrested on Palm Sunday, 1574, for saying Mass in Lady Brown's house in Cow Lane, and was " convicted and had the law according to statute in that case provided " (Ed. 1808, IV, 324).

In Thomas's case, as in William's, an association with Essex is suggested. Moreover, the Manor of Brookhall is only a mile from Tiptree and not far from Witham, places which are both named in the play of *Wether* in the list that ends with " Ynge . . . Butsbery ".

We now come to the fourth of the brothers, John Heywood, the dramatist.

A letter to Lord Burleigh, dated 18th April, 1575, three years before his death, fixes 1497 as the year of Heywood's birth, and it deserves to be printed in full :

Right Honorable, and my verie good Lord : I understand of late what a good earnest sewtor, it hath pleased my good honorable Ladie, your good wiffe, to be for me, nowe in my poore old age, when my frendes are in a manner all dead, and manie of them utterlie forsaken me and my wholle lyvyng

---

[1] It is important to notice that this was not an expression of royal favour, except in so far as an act of justice may be so considered. Heywood only recovered his lease at an enhanced rent.

detayned from me, and the chieffest parte of it, whiche was a
lease for yeares, in Romney Marshe, begged, and bought away
utterlie from me; And neither of that, nor of the rest, not one
pennye of it, paid, or sent hither unto me, for my maintennance
for these twoo yeares, and a half: And (nowe) [1] it pleaseth
you[r] good Lordshippe as I heare, to comaund my sonne Doonne,
to send me over the arreragcs, whiche hath bein deteyned from
me, I beseche god reward, and blesse the quenes hignes and
your good honor for it, as also my good ladie, who hath ever
bene my good Ladie, and nowe my speciall good Ladie, / *And
thowghe Beggars maye not be chusers, yet they may be cravers*, I
will moost humblie therefore crave of the quenes Magestie, and
desyr moost humblie your honour and my good Ladie, to be
sewtors for me, to her magestie, that I may enjoye the rest of
my poore lyvyng, here quietlie, by her highnes lycence and
pattent to me and my assignes, duryng my liffe, which can not
be, by all lykeliehoode above twoo or three yeares, being nowe
lxxviij years of age. / And I will god willing your honor shall
never heare anie otherwise of me than becometh a poore honest
quyett old man, but will spend my tyme, that I have to lyve,
in prayer, and in loking to my last ende, whiche cannot be longe,
seing my hearing begynneth to fayle me, and my myrth decayeth
with age, and my bodie is weake. And I beseech your good
honor, and my good Ladie, to appoynte some one of the
officers of the escheker, or whom it pleaseth your honor,
that maye help my dowghter Marvin that I may have my
Arrerages that is dewe, since I was procleymed, quietlie and
spedelie paid, and sent unto me. And also some order to
enjoye the rest of my poore lyvyng, except my lease, that is
begged and bought away whollie frome me, whiche I dare not
crave, whiche was the verie chefe of my lyvyng: and nowe I
have no maner of benefit of it, whiche I thinke the quene's
magestie never ment, when it was bowght frome me by Justice
Manhoode (Manwood?) and sold by him to my sonne Doonn,
who never sent me one penye yet either of that lease or (of
anie [2]) of my lyving since the tyme he bought my lease, for
he sayth he durst not. / Yf your good honor obteyne not the
pattent to my self and to my assignes, that so I may boldlie
take some order, for the payment of such lyvyng and arrerages,
unto me, as it shall please the quenes magestie, by your honores
and my good ladies sewte, to assigne unto me for my maintennance here duryng my short liffe, I am greatlie affraid, it

---

[1] Correction in Heywood's hand.   [2] Heywood's hand.

will not come spedelie, and whollie to my handes to helpe me, but when I am dead, *whiche is a day (at the least) after the faire.*

Thus I besech god, to preserve the quenes highnes, your good honor and my good ladie, who helpeth me nowe at this great pynche, with my humble dewtie, with daylie prayers and moost humble thanks unto your honor, for the same. And god willing I wilbe both your honors poor beadesman. / From Mechlyne where I have bein sore sacked and spoyled of a good parte of that littill that I had, both by spanyards and Germayns soldiars, *which hath made my purse bare.* And therefore good my Lord, *help to comfort it agayne.* / This xviijth of Aprell i. 5. 7. 5. /

[1] your honors most hombyll orator
as he ys greately bownden

JHON HEYWOOD.

(R.O.S.P. Dom. Eliz.)

The reference to his " mirth " as decaying with age is pathetic, as indeed also are the proverbs, which I have italicized, but they show something of the indomitable, —or shall we say incorrigible ?—spirit of the " Merryman ".[2]

" My good ladie " is Mildred, one of the three scholarly daughters of Sir Anthony Cooke, and wife of Lord Treasurer Burleigh. Ascham held her to be the foremost Greek scholar among the women of her day, saving always his favourite, Lady Jane Grey. Sir Anthony, tutor to Edward VI, was of Gidea Hall, Romford, and Romford, the " capital " of the ancient Royal Liberty of Havering atte Bower,[3] was half-way from London to Ingatestone, where Wm. Heywood would leave the old Roman road to reach his home at " Ynge Gyngiang Jayberd, parish of Butsbery ", which lay three miles off to the south.

If John Heywood was already seventy-eight in April 1575, in April 1509, when Henry VIII came to the throne, he was twelve years old, an age at which a chorister's voice is beginning to be quite well developed. It has been thought that Heywood was a chorister of the Chapel Royal. Sir A. W.

---

[1] In Heywood's hand.   [2] See *Heywood's Proverbs*, pp. 20, 29 (ed. Farmer).
[3] John Clement had a country house near Havering (see *Library*, March 1926).

omits all reference to it.   I give the items as they occur in
Misc. Bk., T.R. No. 216 :

p. 120. *Quarter Wages due Michaelmas* (1519).
         Item Vincent Vulpe painter   100/-
         Item for John Haywoode qrtor wages at xxli.
           by the yere   100/-
p. 140. *Quarter Wages at Christmas Ao XI* (1519)
         Item Vincent Vulpe   100/-
         Item for John Haywoode wages   100/-
p. 162. *Yet Quarter wages due at Ester Ao XI* (1519–20)
         Vyncent Vulp   100/-
         Item for John Hawode wages   100/-
p. 192. *Yet Quarter wages due at Mydsom'* (1520)
         Vincent Vold (?)   100/-
         Item for John Haywode wages   100/-
p. 210. *Yet Quarter wages due at Michell. Ao* 12 (1520)
         Item for Vincent Voulp payntr wages   100/-
         Item for John Haywode synger wages   100/-
p. 231. *Yet Quarter wages due at Christmas Ao* 12 (1520)
         Item for Vincent Vulp paynter   100/-
         Item for John Haywode the synger wages   100/-

It will be noticed that the first record of payment on p. 120
differs from the subsequent items in stating the annual salary,
a fact which points to this being actually the first payment
of the series.   Indeed, seeing that the King's Book is un-
broken from 1506 to 1520–1, it is safe to conclude that we
have here John Heywood's first Court payment.   I would
add that the payments of the preceding quarter (p. 99)
show Vincent Vulp as usual, but not John Heywood.

We saw that at the age of twelve Heywood was not a
chorister of the Chapel Royal.   Apparently at no time was
he a Gentleman of the Chapel.   A Choir of twenty-five
of the Gentlemen accompanied the Court to Guisnes in the
summer of 1520 for the Field of the Cloth of Gold, but Haywood was not among them.   One of the singing men, Thomas
Farthing, present at Guisnes, died on the 8th December,
1520, in the same year.   He had held an annuity of 10 marks
from the issues of the manors of Torpull and Makesey
in Northamptonshire.   This annuity was granted to John

Heywood " during our pleasure " on 12th February, 1520–1 (Privy Seal Warr. No. 499) " in consideracione boni et fidelis servicie quod serviens noster Johes Haywode, etc."

Some irregularity in the form of the warrant led to the issue of a fresh patent in the following April.

Hence it comes about that when the King's Book accounts open again for the isolated Quarterly Michaelmas payments of 1525 they show :

Item to John Heywood player of the virginals £6. 13. 4d.

This new sum of £6 13s. 4d. was probably his regular quarterly wage from the time of Farthing's death, and was made up of his earlier salary of £5 a quarter and the quarter of his annuity of 10 marks. I do not, therefore, feel able to accept Dr. Wallace's statement that this item of £6 13s. 4d. was a fee for some special occasion (*Evolution*, p. 78 n.). It occurs among the quarterly payments just like the series of payments of £5. The apparent isolation is due to the fact that the manuscript is a fragment containing only one quarter's accounts. Dr. Wallace appears to follow Collier in misdating this payment 1526 (see p. 91 n.).

The cost of the French war led to a rigorous overhauling of the expenses of the Royal Household in 1525, when the famous Statutes of Eltham were issued. A number of the royal servants were " discharged out of the King's Court " on annuities or pensions, and the " rate of entertainment of such as shall be discharged " is given as £10 a year for *generosi*, or gentlemen (L. & P. IV, i, p. 871).

Thus in the accounts of the Cofferer of the Household for 1525–6 (R.O., Accounts 41/913), under the head " Annuities ", we have the following items :

Massy viliard and 12 others (*generosi* whose names are
  given)   £10 per annum
23 " Valecti nuper hospicii " (yeomen of the Household)
                                          £6 per annum
28 " garciones nuper de hospicio " (grooms of the Household),
  among whom is a John Heywood [1]   £4 per annum

[1] I assume that this is the recipient of the special payment on 21st January, 1514–15.

It appears that in 1528 Heywood was so " discharged
from the King's Court ", for by a fresh warrant dated 8th
November, 1528, he was granted an " annuell pencion " of
£10 a year for life, and this payment appears in the quarterly
statements of the existing books for 1528–31, 1538–41,
1545 and 1547–51 (see p. 39).

Heywood only held his annuity of 10 marks " during
pleasure ", and there is no patent, so far as I know, to show
the nature of his office as " singer " at £20 a year. This,
too, was obviously held " during pleasure ". We may
conclude, I think, therefore, that Heywood enjoyed a
salary of £20 a year from 1519 to 1520–1, when it was
increased to £26 13s. 4d. by the reversion of Farthing's
annuity of 10 marks ; and that this was his salary until
he was " discharged " on a pension in 1528, and is so shown
on the only existing record as being paid in 1525 in the
regular quarterly payments.

It appears, therefore, that Heywood's first period of
activity at Court began in the summer of 1519 and continued until 1528, and that he was actively engaged at
Court between the ages of twenty-two and thirty-
one.

It will be seen that my results differ very materially
from those given by Dr. Wallace (*Evolution*). He seems to
follow Collier in accepting the payment to the yeoman in
1514–15 as the first recorded payment to the dramatist, as
he follows him in misdating it ; and he omits all reference
to the very important series of payments beginning in 1519.
This omission is the more strange in view of his criticism of
Collier's use of the same manuscripts : " Fragmentary ex-
tracts from both books (King's Books of Payments, Vols.
215–16), chiefly notable for omissions, wholly unreliable
and worthless for reference, are in Collier, I, 76–9 " (*Evolution*, p. 37, n. 3).

Dr. Wallace treats the payment of £6 13s. 4d. in 1525
as " a special fee for some occasion ", although it occurs
in an ordinary set of quarterly payments, and he dates his

regular salary from 1528. I feel that he has attached a false importance to his discovery of the connected series of three patents dealing with Heywood's pension. The first of these I have noted as granting an annuity of £10 on 8th November, 1528, the second substituted for this a pension of £40 vacant by the death of Sir Wm. Penyson on 4th March, 1552, and the third increased it to £50 on 5th April, 1555. Dr. Wallace found that the first two patents were mentioned in the third, and appears to have concluded that they gave the whole history of Heywood's " regular salary ". Further, by a mistranslation of this third patent he extended, as we shall see, the period of his office of Sewer of the Chamber from six years to thirty (*Evolution*, p. 78 n.).

Whereas, however, Dr. Wallace thus treats the year 1528 as marking the beginning of Heywood's career as Court dramatist, I suggest that it marks the close of his first period of Court favour.

The entry of the first payment of the " pencion " occurs on f. 11 in the accounts for 1528–31 (R.O., Misc. Bks., Q.R., 420/11). The book opens on 1st October, and the first set of quarterly payments follows at Christmas. The entry reads :

> Item to John Haywood upon warrant dated the viii day of November aᵒ XXᵒ for his annuell pencion after the rate of Xli by the yere to be paide unto hym quarterly from the feast of Saint Mighell last past by evyn porcions during his lyf as aperᵗʰ in the same warrant   50/-

The fact that he was pensioned does not mean that Heywood's connection with the Court ceased, although his affairs now lay principally elsewhere. He appears in the list of recipients of the King's New Year's Gifts in January 1532–3, and this implies that he had also given a gift to the King. One thinks of Sebastian Westcott's New Year's Gift to Queen Mary of a " book of ditties, written ", and wonders whether Heywood gave to the King a manuscript copy of his plays that Rastell printed during the following year. The gift is entered thus :

> To Heywood. Item a gilte cuppe with a couer weing XXIII oz. (S.P. Hen. VIII, N. (1).)[1]

Except for the performance in 1539 of Cromwell's *Masque of King Arthur's Knights*, this is the only reference I have found to Heywood at Court during the years 1528–52. The Lord Chamberlain's Accounts support the view that he was not, during this period, an active servant, for whilst he was granted full livery for himself and two servants as Sewer of the Chamber at the funeral of Edward VI, under whom he had succeeded to Sir Wm. Penyson's pension of £40, he was not mentioned in the accounts of Henry VIII's funeral (L.C. 2/2) nor of the coronation of Edward VI (L.C. 2/3), when his pension was £10. Similarly, having definitely retired on 12th November, 1558, he does not appear in the accounts of Mary's funeral (L.C. 9, 5 (2)), nor of the coronation of Elizabeth (L.C. 9/4). The Lord Chamberlain's accounts at the Record Office do not contain an account of Mary's coronation, but the Wardrobe Warrants [2] show that he had his livery for the ceremony as a Sewer of the Chamber. The fact is that he became an honorary Sewer of the Chamber, *dapifer camerae*, and so was entitled to his livery, between 4th March, 1551–2, and Edward's death, 6th July, 1553.[3]

---

[1] See p. 78.   [2] R.O., Exchequer Accounts, 427/5.

[3] The patent issued by Philip and Mary on 5th April, 1555, states clearly that the earlier annuities of 1528 and 1551–2 were granted to Heywood *per nomen dilecti servientis nostri*, but that now (*modo*) he was *dapifer camerae*. The patent reads : " Rex et Regina omnibus, &c. . . . cum percharissimus pater noster . . . Henricus nuper Rex Anglie per billam suam signatam sub sigillo suo manuali datam octavo die novembris anno regni sui vicisimo dederit et concesserit delecto servienti nostro Johanni Heywood Generoso *modo* uni dapiferorum camerae nostrae *per nomen dilecti servientis* quandam annuitatem . . . decem librarum per annum &c. . . . Cumque etiam percharissimus frater noster . . . Edwardus nuper Res Angliae sixtus per litteras suas patentes datas apud Westministerium quarto die Martii Anno Regni sui sixto dederit et concesserit prefato Johanni Heywood *per nomen delecti ac fidelis servientes sui Johannis Heywood* quandam annuitatem . . . quadraginta librarum."

It is probable that Heywood was married in 1523, for in that year he was admitted to the Freedom of the City on request by letter from the King, and took up his residence in the City.

The Town Clerk's Records at the Guildhall show that in the Mayoralty of Mundy the Common Council refused to admit the King's servant, John Heywood, to the Freedom, " except he pay the new hanse of £10 according to the new Act " (3rd March, 1522–3). At a Common Council, however, on 22nd May, 1523, " at the contemplacion of the Kynges letter, John Heywoode ys admitted into the liberties of this citie, payinge the olde hanse " (Letter Book N, ff. 222 and 239). Similar entries occur in the Journals.[1]

As admission to the Freedom was either by Patrimony, Apprenticeship, Gift, or Redemption, it appears that Heywood had no claim by Patrimony, and that he was, therefore, not born of London parents.[2]

An item in the Town Clerk's Records of 5th May, 1521, (Repertories 5, f. 284) is of value as showing the activities of Heywood's father-in-law, John Rastell, at that period :

It is agreed by the Courte that the pageante devised by Rastell to stond at the litell conduyte by the stokkes shall go forth and take effect, so alwey that the charge thereof exceed not XV li.

The " litell conduyte " stood at the east end of the Church of St. Michael in the Querne in Cheapside, near Paul's Gate, where Rastell's shop stood " at the Sign of the Mermaid ".

In the previous summer Rastell had been engaged in preparing the magnificent hall for the Field of the Cloth of Gold.

John Heywood married Rastell's daughter, Joan. In her brother William's will the first-named daughter of John Heywood is Joanna Stubbs. Now, in the Trinity term,

[1] The jealousy with which the City guarded its privileges is shown by an entry in 1518 : " The letter of Maister Richard Pace, the Kynges secretary, for his brother to be admitted to be made freeman of the city was reade and the said counsell would in no wyse agree therto."

[2] See pp. 29–30 on Heywood's parentage.

1542, John Heywood and Joan, his wife, and Christopher Stubbe [1] and Joan, his wife, jointly conveyed to Wm. Rastell for a payment of £200 property in Tottenham consisting of two messuages of 60 acres of land, 40 acres of meadows, 60 acres of pasture, and 20 acres of marsh, *cum pertinentibus* (Feet of Fines, 34 Hen. VIII, 27/184).

I imagine, therefore, that Joan Stubbs, Heywood's daughter, thus took her dowry and marriage settlement, being then newly married at the age, say, of eighteen ; and I assume that Heywood's admission to the Freedom of the City in 1523 implies that he was married then and became a householder in the City. It was probably through the influence of his father-in-law, John Rastell, that he was admitted a member of the Stationers' Company.

From the age, therefore, of about twenty-five Heywood was a citizen of London, and his association with the City became intimate and official. In Letter Book O of the Town Clerk's Records at the Guildhall occurs an entry hitherto unnoticed :

20 Die Januarii. Dodmer Maier. (1529–30).

John Heywood citizen and Stacyoner of London and oon of the kynges serauntes ys presented by Maister Rauff Warren Maister Wardeyn of the Mercers to this Courte as Comen Mesurer or meter of lynnen Clothes to occupie by hym or his sufficient depute and to doe Right and equally betwene all parties. And also he ys transmuted from the saide craft of Stacyoner unto the mistery of Mercers by thassent of bothe the saide mestares.

This record is interesting for several reasons. It shows that Heywood, having been put on the list of life annuitants by the Crown in 1528—a substantial privilege—was welcomed a year later by the foremost of the London Livery Companies. It supports my contention that Heywood's first period of Court activity culminated rather than began in 1528. Further, it is noteworthy that 1529 was the year in which

---

[1] Son of a Prothonotary of the Common Pleas—another link with legal circles.

More became Chancellor, and More's influence in the City was very considerable.[1]

Pitseus describes John Heywood as for many years most intimate with Sir Thomas More, and since More died on 5th July, 1535, the term *multis annis familiarissimus* must mean that Heywood was one of the young people More loved to have about him.

A consideration of dates suggests that Heywood had been introduced to the Court by More. His first quarterly payment in 1519 shows that his appointment dates from Midsummer, and it was on 23rd July of that year that More gave up his office as Under-Sheriff, which he had held since 1510, and became absorbed at Court.[2]

The process of absorption had been gradual. Already, before the publication of *Utopia* in 1516, he had attracted Wolsey's notice; in 1518 he was Master of Requests and a Privy Councillor, and in 1520 he was present at the Field of the Cloth of Gold; in 1521 he was knighted and made Sub-Treasurer; in 1522 and 1525 large grants of lands were made to him; in 1523 he was Speaker; in June 1525, he took a prominent part in the pageants at the creation of Henry's natural son as Duke of Richmond (Brewer, II, 102), and in July he was made Chancellor of the Duchy of Lancaster. He succeeded Wolsey as Chancellor in 1529 and resigned in 1532.

The case of John Clement, More's brilliant son-in-law, may be instanced as an illustration or parallel of Heywood's.

---

[1] Another instance of More's influence in the City in 1529 may be alluded to : " At this courte Sir Thomas More Chauncelir of the Ducye of Lancaster recommended oon Water Smyth nowe his servaunte and hath contynued wt hym by the space of viii or ix yeres to the Rowme of the Swerde berer yn stede and place of Richard Berwyk late nowe decessed . . . et postea . . . Walterus admissus fuit " (Letter Book O, f. 168b). This is the Walter Smyth who wrote the *Twelve Merry Gests of the Widow Edyth*, printed by John Rastell in 1525.

[2] It may be significant that the year 1519 witnessed a reform of the Household which caused some comment at the time. The King removed from the Court " divers that were his minions and of his chamber . . . and the bruit was that they after their appetite governed the King " (L. & P., 20th May, 1519). Henry was twenty-eight years of age.

Clement was present (with Peter Giles) at the birth of *Utopia* in the garden at Antwerp. In 1518 Erasmus alludes to his being in attendance on the Cardinal (L. & P., 10 Hen. VIII), and warns him against studying at night, suggesting that he learn to write standing while on duty. Next year he was Wolsey's lecturer in Rhetoric at Oxford and Reader in Greek. In 1520 More tells Erasmus that Clement has taken up Medicine and resigned his Readership to Lupset [1] (L. & P., 12 Hen. VIII). Thomas Linacre, friend of More and Erasmus, had founded the College of Physicians in 1518 at his own house, the " Stone-house in Knight Rider Street " (Roll of R.C.P. by W. Monk, 1878). In 1525 Clement is described in the Eltham Statutes as a " Sewer of the Chamber, out of wages ", and in the same year he appears in the King's Book of Payments (Eg. 2604) :

Item John Clement, exibiceo ultra mare, £10.

When the King's Book re-opens in 1528 he is in regular half-yearly receipt of £10 as " Phisicon ", and this payment is recorded in the existing books up to 1540, when he drops out of the accounts.

He had been elected a Fellow of the College of Physicians in February 1528, and in the following year he was sent by the King to see Wolsey at Esher, where he was already suffering from his last illness.

The year 1519, from which I date Heywood's career at Court, was also, as we have seen, an important one for his future father-in-law, and a consideration of the activities of More, Clement and John Rastell and their close and familiar relationship seems to warrant one in concluding that Heywood entered upon his life at Court as one of their circle. His known loyalty to the memory of More, perhaps, tends to obscure the influence of his versatile and energetic father-in-law, John Rastell. It should, however, be borne in mind that at a very impressionable age he must have

---

[1] " Successit enim (Lupsetus) Joanni Clementi meo, nam is se totum addixit rei Medicae."—More to Erasmus (More's Latin Works, Basle, 1563).

been closely interested in his numerous schemes and under-takings.

The years immediately preceding 1519 Heywood had probably spent at Oxford. His name does not appear in the printed Registers, but there is nothing improbable in Anthony à Wood's account of the matter: " He laid the foundation of learning in this University, particularly as it seems in that ancient hostel called Broadgates in St. Aldate's parish ; but the crabbedness of logic not suiting with his airy genie, he retired to his native place, and became noted to all witty men, especially to Sir Thomas More ". It may be noted that the numerous woodcuts in the *Spider and the Flie* (1556) show the author in what Sir A. W. Ward describes as an M.A. gown (*D.N.B.*), and further, that he is described in Wm. Rastell's will as " Dominus ", possibly as an academic title, although it is also applicable to the lord of a manor (Martin's *Record Interpreter*, p. 197).

His contemporaries certainly did not consider Heywood a scholar. In 1548 Bale wrote of him :

Johannes Heywode, ut Orpheus alter, instrumentorum studiosus, musica et poeta, habebat in sua lingua gratiam (*Scriptorum*, Ipswich ed.).

In 1557 he says more emphatically that he was " in sua lingua studiosus ac sine doctrina ingeniosus ".

Pitseus in 1619 wrote : " Johannes Heywodus, Thomae Moro multis annis familiarissimus, vir pius, utcumque doctus valde ingeniosus . . . et in familiari colloquio lepidus atque facetus ". He adds, however, that he had his sons thoroughly grounded *in bonis litteris*. Pitts knew Jasper Heywood well : " Gasparum Romae primum, deinde Neapoli familiariter novi ".

I think that some light may be thrown on Heywood's connection with Oxford when we learn more of his friendship with William Forrest, afterwards Chaplain to Queen Mary.

In 1544–5 Forrest dedicated to Wm. Parr, Earl of Essex,

E

a poem in " simple royal metre ", on *The History of the Patriarch Joseph.* He protests that he has not the " flourishing vein of Gower's phrase "; " flowers of rhetoric " he never gathered, and as for learning, " Heywood and I be near one ". He praises him (" my friend Heywood "), however, " for the conveyance of a fine sentence " (Add. MS. 34791).

Forrest was an enthusiastic musician, and left behind him a very valuable collection of contemporary music, now at Oxford and known as the " Forrest-Heyther " Collection, consisting of six part-books written in 1530 by (or for) Forrest (Davey, *Hist. Eng. Mus.*, p. 98).

It seems that in the " simple and unlearned Sir William Forrest, Preiste ", we have an Oxford musician whose academic position is not unlike Heywood's.

It appears from his poem on Queen Katherine (" The Second Gresield ") that Forrest knew Christ Church, Oxford, in 1530, and Warton says that he had a Christ Church pension of £6 in 1555 (Hazlitt's *Warton*, iv, 231).

In 1521 Heywood not only received the annuity of 10 marks, but had hopes of an important grant of the manor of Haydon, one of the manors of the Duke of Buckingham, who had been executed on 17th May, 1521. The manor is situated on the north-west border of Essex. Our only legal authority for the grant, so far as I know, is a legal commonplace book in which a copy of the draft enrolment occurs (Add. MS. 24844). The grant is made out to Heywood and his heirs male " in consideracione veri et fidelis servicii ", but it was not confirmed.

Heywood's grants and payments from the Crown may, perhaps, be most conveniently considered together. They are :

1. Wages at £20 per ann. to " John Heywood, Singer," from Michaelmas, 1519.
2. Annuity of 10 marks " during pleasure " from 8 Dec. 1520.
3. Pension for life of £10 a year from Michaelmas, 1528. (Terms of Warrant given Xmas 1528 in Excheq.

Q.R. 420/11). 1 and 2 now cease and a regular quarterly payment of 50/- to "John Heywood, Player of the Virginals," takes their place.

4. Recovery of his Manor of Brookhall, near Tiptree in Essex, on the assent and recommendation of the Court of Augmentation, for 21 years at a rent of £14. 1. 6. (1540) (see p. 35).

5. Pension of £40 vacant by the death of Sir Wm. Penyson ; granted 4th March, 1552, by Edward VI in place of the old pension of £10 (Ct. of Aug., Enrolt. of Leases, 6 Ed. VI). Becomes *dapifer camerae*.[1]

6. Reversion of leases in Romney Marsh [2] (Pat. Roll., 1 and 2 P. & M.). These lands are fully described later from an Inquisition held 14 Eliz., Heywood being then described as living at Hinxwell, Kent (near Ashford). (202½ acres at £45 17s. 0d. per annum.)

7. Pension increased to £50 in 1555 (Pat. Roll, 1 and 2 P. & M., Pt. 4). This enrolment, as Dr. Wallace notes, mentions the two earlier amounts of the pension (£10 on 8th Nov., 1528, and £40 on 4th March, 1552) and records in the margin its final cancellation on 12th Nov., 1558, under the terms of the next grant.

8. The manor of Bulmer and other lands in Bulmer and Belborne, near Malton, Yorks, belonging to Sir John Bulmer, recently attainted of High Treason. This grant was made 12th Nov., 1558, five days before Mary's death, and marks Heywood's retirement from the Royal service.

An examination of the dates of these grants confirms my earlier statement that Heywood had two well-defined periods of activity at Court, the first from 1519 to 1528, the second from the reign of Edward VI to the close of Mary's reign. It is to the second period that Puttenham refers : "Afterward in King Edward the sixth's time came to be in reputation for the same facultie ('vulgar makyngs') . . John Heywood the Epigrammatist who for the myrth and quicknesse of his conceite more than for any good learning was in him came to be well benefitted by the king" (Arber's ed., p. 74).

---

[1] "Sewer of the Chamber."
[2] Forfeited to the Crown by Sir Thomas Wyatt.

It was probably while More and Rastell were in prison
that Heywood began the *Spider and the Flie*. He published
it in 1556, but it was begun twenty years before :

> I have (good readers) this parable here pende :
> (After olde beginning) newly brought to ende.
> The thing, yeres mo then twentie since it begoon.
> To the thing : yeres mo then ninetene, nothing doon.
>   *Spider and Flie*. (The Conclusion.)

The work had been untouched for at least twenty years,
and was begun earlier. I think there are good reasons for
supposing that John Rastell was the original " flie " and
Cranmer the spider.

In 1534 Heywood wrote the ballad to Princess Mary, *Give
place ye ladies*, which is found in Tottel's Miscellany, where
it is printed without the last two quatrains :

> This worthye ladye to beewraye
> A kinges daughter was she
> Of whom John Heywood lyste to say
> In such worthy degree.

> And Marye was her name weete yee
> With these graces indude
> At eighteen yeares so flourisht shee
> So doth his meane conclude.

This fuller version appears in Harl., 1703, a book of poems
mostly by Heywood's friend, William Forrest, " the symple
and unlearned priest " (see p. 49).

Mary was born on 18th February, 1515–16, and it is
significant of Heywood's sympathies that this ballad was
written within a year or so of the divorce, and soon after
Mary had been declared illegitimate.

Sir A. W. Ward (*D.N.B.*, art. Heywood) says that " the
opening and the prettiest passages of the poem are borrowed
from Surrey " ; but as Surrey was born in 1517, according to
the inscription on the Arundel portrait, it is more likely
that he borrowed from Heywood.

As a musician, Heywood appears to have been associated

with John Redford, of St. Paul's, the composer of instrumental music and writer of plays.

The signatures or "Acknowledgements of Supremacy" taken in 1534 are collected and printed in Deputy Keeper's Report, 7, App. 2, pp. 279–336, and among the six Vicars-Choral or singing men of St. Paul's we find Redford's name. In his will (P.C.C. 50, Alen), which was proved in 1547, Redford describes himself as " oon of the Vicars of the Cathedral Church of Saynt Paule and maister of the Almerie there ".[1] His sole executor and residuary legatee was his successor, Sebastian Westcott, " oon of the vicars of powles ".

One of the most valuable collections of Tudor instrumental music, the famous " Mulliner " book (Add. MS. 30513), contains a considerable amount of Redford's best work,[2] and it is made more interesting by the inscription on the first flyleaf, in a suspiciously stiff hand :

> Sum liber thomae Mullineri
> iohanne heywoode teste.

It is a small oblong book in an original binding with rolled border of conventional ornaments alternating with the port-cullis, rose, fleur-de-lys and the letters H.R. A similar binding at the Record Office is described by Weale (No. 191), and I believe it occurs again on the Eton College MS., which Davey (p. 89) describes as the most important of the musical remains of Henry VII. This last book was almost certainly written originally for Eton. The " Mulliner " binding has, so far as I know, not been authoritatively described.

Mulliner's compositions are well known, but little is known of him, except that he is said to have been at St. Paul's (*D.N.B.*). He appears from the inscription above to have been Heywood's pupil and under him to have collected a

[1] As Thomas Hyckman, Redford's predecessor as " Master of the Almerie " (i.e. Master of the Paul's Boys), died in 1534, we may date Redford's period of office 1534–47. Redford was succeeded by Westcott.

[2] This was a period of English pre-eminence in music. The Chapel Royal attracted a remarkable concentration of musical talent, but the great composer of instrumental music under Henry VIII was John Redford of St. Paul's (Davey, *Hist. Eng. Mus.* (1895), pp. 141 and 166).

humorous lament of the "poore syllye boyes", with the refrain :

> Of all the creatures / lesse and moe
> We lytle poore boyes / abyde much woe.
> Wee have a cursyd master / I tell you all for trew
> so cruell as he is was never turk nor Jew
> he is the most unhappiest man / that ever ye knewe
> for to poore syllye boyes / he wurkyth ev^r much woe.

This song-book seems to be a St. Paul's collection. Redford's work and Heywood's form the greater part of it, and it is clear that the collection was still being added to in Westcott's time.

"Sebastian, scolemaister of Powles, gave queen Mary on New Year's Day, 1557, a book of ditties written " (Nichols' *Progresses*, I, xxxv.). Perhaps, if this book came to light, it would be found to be based upon this repertory of St. Paul's songs.[1] Mulliner's book remains to show, if his signature is genuine, that he was one of Heywood's most gifted pupils, but there was at least one other who was more distinguished, for in January 1536–7 there occurs the entry in Princess Mary's Book of Expenses (Royal 17 B, xxviii, f. 7b) :

Item given to Heywood's servant for bringing my lady graces Regalles to Greenwich xx^d.

and a year later on, f. 42 of the same MS., is the item, March 1537–8 :

to Heywood playing an interlude with his children before my lady grace xls (40/-).

The question has often been raised as to who Heywood's children were, and as this is the earliest reference to them, it may be useful to deal now with all the known references together. They are five in number :

1. The reference given above, which simply calls them " his children ".

---

[1] The Interlude and poems of Add. MS. 15233 were printed for the Shakespeare Society by Halliwell Phillipps in 1848.

2. In 1551, 13th February, the Household Expenses of Princess Elizabeth (Camden, Misc. II) show the entry :

Paid in rewarde to the Kinges maiesties dromer and phiphe 20/- ; Mr Heywoode 30/- ; and to Sebastian towards the charge of the children with the carriage of the plaiers garments £4. 19. 0. In thole as by warraunte appereth £7. 9. 0.

As this is one charge paid under a single warrant it points to one entertainment rather than three separate ones as Dr. Wallace prefers to read it, and it suggests Heywood's collaboration with Westcott and the Paul's children.

3. In 1552 the Revels Accounts from Loseley MSS. (ed. Feuillerat, 1914) show

a play of the state of Ireland and another of children set out by Mr Heywood.

In this instance twelve coats are paid for " for the children ", and, as the number of the children of the Chapel Royal was twelve and this series of entertainments was under the control of George Ferrers and the Office of the Revels, it seems probable that these were the boys of the Chapel.   In Colet's time the number of boys under the Almoner of Paul's was eight (Sparrow Simpson, *Reg. Stat.*, p. 234), but in Sebastian Westcott's time there were ten.

4. Mary's progress through the City from the Tower to Westminster, an occasion of much pageantry.   Stowe's *Annals* (p. 617) says :

Then she rode forth (from Cheapside) and in Paul's Churchyard against the School (Colet's foundation at the East end of the Cathedral) one Master Haywood sate in a pageant under a vine and made to her an oration in Latin and in English.

Then after an account of a feat by Peter the Dutchman who performed on the steeple, Stowe adds :

Then there was a pageant made against the Dean of Paul's Gate (on the S.W. side of the Cathedral) where the choristers of Paul's played on vialls and sung.

Heywood's pageant is more particularly described in the *Chronicle of the Gray Friars* (Camden Soc., p. 82 n.) as " a pageant in Powlles Churcheyard at the est ende of the church, and there she stode longe for it was made of rosemary withall her armes and a crowne in the myddes ".

A third description occurs in the *Chronicle of Queen Jane and Queen Mary* (Camden Soc., p. 30, and Harl. 194) :

At the Scholehouse in Palles church ther was certayn children and men sung dyverse staves in gratifying the quene ; ther she stayed a goode while and gave diligent ere to their song.

Here we have two distinct pageants, Heywood's at the east end, at St. Paul's school, thrice recorded, and particularly honoured by the Queen's especial notice ; and the pageant by the Paul's children (at the Dean's Gate) near the Almerie.

Heywood has here a choir of men and boys who were not from St. Paul's, and this pageant was probably a tribute from Colet's School, staged, managed and augmented by Heywood, who also read the Latin encomium and perhaps composed the English one.

5. In Machyn's Diary under the date August 1559, occurs the last recorded reference to Heywood's dramatic activities in a description of the entertainments provided for Elizabeth at Nonsuch :

a playe of ye chyldren of powlls and ther master S(ebastian), Mr Phelypes and Mr Haywode, and after a gret banket.

References of dramatic interest in Machyn have to be examined, as the manuscript has been tampered with in some cases, but this entry is quite clean. The full name Sebastian is taken from Strype, who used the manuscript before it suffered from the Cotton fire.

Here again we have an undoubted instance of Heywood's association with Westcott and the Paul's boys, and from what has already been said of Westcott's predecessor, John

Redford, as a musician and writer of plays, it is probable that the connection was one of long standing.

Thus, of five references, two are definitely to the Paul's children, one may be to Colet's foundation, one is possibly to the Chapel children, and the earliest is quite uncertain, although at the time Heywood was associated with Redford.

On the whole, I think the evidence points to Heywood being associated with St. Paul's or " called in " there and elsewhere, to manage, collaborate, or advise. He was the author or joint author of plays and the deviser or joint deviser of pageants, and where so much is uncertain we can at least, I think, postulate his association with Redford and Westcott.

Dr. Wallace's statement, therefore, appears to need reconsideration :

Heywood is not known to have written for or to have been in any way associated with any other children's company than the Children of the Chapel. His services as sewer of the chamber, singer, musician and general entertainer were retained at Court by Henry VIII, Edward VI and Queen Mary on regular fees as well as by annuities and royal manorial grants. It is not likely therefore, as has been generally guessed, that he ever wrote for the Paul's boys, although seven of his songs and ballads probably intended to be sung in interludes were collected by his friend John Redford, former master of Paul's in a MS. containing Redford's own interlude of *Wit and Science.*— (*Evolution.*)

I have already shown that there is no evidence of Heywood's activity at Court between 1528 and 1552, although he appears to have been a *persona grata* with Princess Mary. The only instance of a Court performance by Heywood during this period was paid for by Cromwell and prepared for him in 1538–9, the year after Heywood's children played before the Princess.

The following items referring to it occur in Cromwell's Book of Accounts (R.O., Excheq., T.R., Misc. Bk., 256) :

11 Feb. (1538–9). Chris. Mylyoner. Payed to him for the

stuf of the maske of king arturs knights £10. 17. 11 and for the labor of workmen £3.

12th Feb.   for necessaries for my Lords maske and also for comfittes when the Lords dyned with my Lorde, £9. 2. 1.

21st Feb.   Payed to the paynter that made all the hobby horses and the other things ther belonging, £33. 17. 6. Heywoode. The same daye payed to him for his costes and other necessaries layed out £6. 10. 5. Mrs Vaughan.   The same day payed to her for certayne things bought of her for the maskes £6. 7. 6.

The 22nd of the same monetht payed to the bargeman that carried Heywoods maske to the courte and home againe, 16/8.

These items all seem to refer to one masque.   The hobby horses were for *King Arthur's Knights*.   It was " Heywood's maske ", and it was performed twice at Cromwell's expense, at his house before 11th February and again at Court before 22nd February.   The items show further that it was a costly and elaborate performance.[1]

On 10th July, 1540, within six months of the performance of the burlesque masque of *King Arthur's Knights*, Cromwell was executed and power fell into the hands of Norfolk, whose sympathies were with the Catholic party.   Attacks were begun upon the Reformer Cranmer, and Heywood became seriously involved in them.   The conspirators imagined that they had in the " Statute of the Six Articles " an instrument that would enable them to convict the Primate of heresy, and, secretly supported by Gardiner, they began to accumulate evidence in Cranmer's own diocese

[1] Cromwell's Accounts show the existence of an extraordinary multiplicity of actors' companies :

Feb. 1536–7.	The Queen's Players (Jane Seymour)	20/–
Dec. 1537.	The King's Players	22/6
,, ,,	The Lord Chamberlain's Players	20/–
,, ,,	The Marquis of Exeter's Players	15/–
Jan. 1537–8.	The Lord Warden's Players	20/–
,, ,,	The Duke of Suffolk's Players	20/–
,, ,,	The Lord Chancellor's Players	10/–
Feb 2nd, 1537–8.	Woodall (Nicholas Udal) the schoolmaster of Eton for playing before my Lord	£5
Feb. 4th, 1537–8.	Lord Cobham's Players	20/–
April 1538.	Mr. Hopton's priest for playing before my Lord with his children	22/6

in Kent. But Henry, who had no intention of sacrificing Cranmer, made him president of the Commission of investigation. Shakespeare tells the story of Cranmer's victory in *Henry VIII*, Act v, Sc. iii.

Several of the conspirators were convicted of treason and condemned to death with forfeiture of their goods and estates, and among these was John Heywood.

Winchester's nephew, German Gardiner, was hanged and quartered on 7th March, 1544, and the same fate befell John Larke, Rector of Chelsea, and other priests. In April John More recanted and was pardoned. Beckinson was pardoned in May, but Heywood remained obdurate, or was kept in suspense till the end of June. On Sunday, 6th July, at Paul's Cross, he read a long and humiliating recantation, robed in a white gown, and received his pardon. I have searched without success at the Record Office for the report of a Commission appointed on the 12th April to take over the estates and goods of the condemned men.

Harington's *Metamorphosis of Ajax* (1596), a satirical and very unpleasant *jeu d'esprit* that offended Elizabeth, has a passage bearing on Heywood's escape from the Tyburn hurdle :

What think you by Haywood that escaped hanging with his mirth ? The king being graciously and (as I think) truly persuaded that a man that wrote so pleasant and harmless verses could not have any harmful conceit against his proceedings ; and so, by the honest motion of a gentleman of his Chamber, saved him from the jerk of the six stringed whip. This Haywood for his proverbs and epigrams is not yet put down by any of our country (Chiswick ed., p. 41).

It was probably while Heywood's case was the talk of London that the *Four PP.* was published. Wm. Middleton, the printer of the play, according to Mr. Duff, began to print in 1542 and he died in 1547 (P.C. Wills, 39, Alen). In any case Heywood certainly did not collapse under his disgrace, for in 1546 Berthelet, the King's printer, published his *Dialogues conteyning the number of the effectual proverbs in the English tounge, compact in a matter concernynge two maner of maryages.*[1] This, together with subsequent collections of six hundred epigrams, was published in 1562 as *John Heywoodes Woorkes*, by Th. Powell. No copy of the *Dialogue* is known to exist, although it was sold at the Roxburghe sale in 1812 (Lowndes). It is also recorded in the Hist. MSS. Commission's Report on the Paget MSS. as appearing in a MS. catalogue written by Lord Stafford in 1556.

The patent enrolling Heywood's pardon refers to him as " late of London, *alias* of North Mymmes." He had bought the lease of a property there, named Iveries, from John Coningsby, Lord of the Manor, on 2nd November, 1540, and in 1542 Wm. Rastell also bought two properties there (Feet of Fines, 1542, Easter and Michaelmas).

North Mymmes was a home of the Mores, who owned the sub-manor named Gobions, the other sub-manor of Brookmans belonging to the Fortescues. Henry Peacham, the author of *The Compleat Gentleman*,[2] says :

Merry John Heywood wrote his Epigrams, as also Sir Thomas More his Utopia, in the parish wherein I was born (North Mims in Hartfordshire, near to St. Albans), where either of them dwelt and had fair possessions.

Peacham was born in 1575, and his evidence may be taken to represent the talk of intelligent people. There is no reason to reject Peacham's statement as to Heywood, but Sir Thomas More never possessed Gobions, for it passed to the widow, Lady Alice, on Sir John More's death. Except for the years 1565–7 the registers of the Church contain no entries earlier than 1662, and there are no memorials

---

[1] On 8th August, 1544, a month after his pardon, a John Heywood appears as a " Captain of the men " serving at the siege of Boulogne. Did Heywood seize this opportunity of re-establishing himself ? John Rastell was similarly engaged in 1512–13.

[2] Dr. Johnson is said to have taken his heraldic definitions from *The Compleat Gentleman.*

relating to either the Mores, Heywoods or Peacham. Whether Heywood had any interest in North Mymmes before he acquired Iveries in 1540 I cannot say. His name does not appear in any Subsidy Roll for the Hundred of Dacorum, and I am inclined to think that his connection arose through the Mores, if it existed at all before 1540.

Ellis Heywood, John's elder son, became a Fellow of All Souls in 1548, and Jasper, then thirteen years of age, is said to have been a page in the household of Princess Elizabeth (*D.N.B.*). I have shown that in 1545, a year after his public humiliation, Heywood was again receiving his quarterly pension of 50s., and he appears to have continued to walk warily through Edward's reign and until his sons were independent. Edward succeeded to the throne on 28th January, 1546–7, and died 7th July, 1553.

In 1552 Heywood was assisting Ferrers and Baldwin in the Court plays, and his pension was increased. In Sir Anthony Cooke and his daughter Mildred, Cecil's wife, he had friends at Court, and it is more than likely that his personality and wit attracted the boy-king. In any case, he probably knew better than many how to amuse him. But it is pathetic to observe the desperate energy with which Northumberland sought to revive the spirits of the young king during his last year. The Loseley MSS. (ed. Feuillerat, 1914) display the short reign closing in a round of plays, pageants and buffoonery. There is a pageant of the Greek Worthies, another of " Medioxes being half death, half man ", another of Bagpipes, another of Cats, another of Tumblers, " a play of the State of Ireland, and another of Children set out by Mr. Heywood,", and " divers other plays and pastymes ".

The introduction to Wm. Baldwin's interesting allegory, " Beware the Cat ", gives a valuable and striking picture of the " devisers " of these entertainments, and the allegory, with its admirable story of the raid of the Irish kern, Patrick Apore, upon Cayer Mackart and how Graymalkin caused his death, points to Baldwin as the maker of

F

the Pageant of Cats as well as the play on Ireland, mentioned above.[1]

In Mary's reign Heywood was in great favour and prosperity. He added to his proverbs and epigrams, and, after an interval of twenty years, he took up again his old allegory of the *Spider and the Flie* and turned it into a complimentary poem to the Queen (see also pp. 34 and 54). His friends, Wm. Rastell, Dr. Clement and Anthony Bonvyse, returned from exile, Rastell to become a judge and Clement to resume his practice ; his son Ellis was attached to the service of Cardinal Pole, and Jasper became a Probationer-Fellow of Merton.

In the last year of Mary's reign (1558) Jasper Heywood was Lord of Misrule at Lincoln's Inn, and he had probably already finished the translation of *Troas*, the first of his three Senecan tragedies. It was published in 1559 by Tottel, who appears from the introduction to *Thyestes* to have annoyed the translator by his indifference to the corrections made in the proofs. *Thyestes*, the second of Jasper Heywood's translations, was published in 1560 from " the hous late Thomas Berthelettes ".[2] In 1561 his third and last translation, *Hercules Furens*, appeared.

Before leaving this subject, further allusion must be made to the Introduction to *Thyestes*. It is dedicated to Sir John Mason, a benefactor of All Souls, a Privy Councillor, a friend of Cecil's (P.C. Wills, 2, Stonard, 1566), and presumably also of the Heywoods (see also p. 35). It shows Jasper Heywood as the associate and admirer of North,

[1] Baldwin, like John Rastell, was a printer and author. His most remarkable work appears to have been the play *Love and Live*, with sixty-two characters, that he offered to the Master of the Revels in Mary's reign. Just as Rastell's device represented the *Four Elements*, Baldwin used the phrase " Love and Live " in his rude printer's device, apparently with reference to his play. He is better known as editor of the *Mirror for Magistrates*. See Miss E. I. Feasey's article in the *Library*, Dec. 1922, and *Mod. Lang. Rev.*, 1925.

[2] Berthelet, who died in 1555, was succeeded by his son-in-law, Thomas Powell, who in the following year published the *Spider and the Flie*, and in 1562 *John Heywoodes Workes*. This accounts for the occurrence in *Thyestes* of the woodcut of Melpomene used several times in the *Spider and the Flie*.

JOHN HEYWOOD
FROM THE MUSEUM COPY OF 'THE SPIDER AND THE FLIE'

Dyall, Sackville, Norton and Yelverton, and he especially speaks of

> Baldwyn's worthy fame
> Whose " Mirror " doth of Magistrates
> Proclaim eternal fame.

He protests to the shade of Seneca, which had visited him as he slumbered over his book on a dull November day, that any of these " Minerva's men " would, in their " stately style ", render Seneca in English much more adequately than he :

> In Lyncoln's Inne and Temples twayne
> Grayes Inne and other mo,
> Thou shalt them finde, whose painful pen
> Thy verse shall flourish so,
> That Melpomen thou wouldst well weene
> had taught them for to wright
> And all their works with stately style
> and goodly grace endight.

This long introduction is artificial, but there breathes in it a buoyant academic spirit. Truly the Tudor world was strangely unstratified. There seems, in terms of modern thought, to be a gulf between this nephew, who can write from experience the lines :

> No princes perfume like to it
> In chamber of estate.

and the uncle, William of Harvard Stock, then living, who left to his widow his kine " to give or discharge the heriots ".

The Elizabethan " Settlement of Religion " drove into exile John Heywood, Wm. Rastell, Dr. Clement, and their wives. Elizabeth had made Parker Primate in 1559 to restore order in discipline and worship. Rome retaliated by prohibiting Catholics from being present at the " new worship ". In 1563 the Articles of Religion were constituted a standard of belief of the Church of England, and in 1564 a Commission was appointed to enforce the Act of Uniformity.

the Earl of Leicester, but Grindal won the day, probably because of Sebastian's position as master of the choristers, for " there is committed unto him the Education of the Choristers or singing children " (Strype's *Grindal*, 1563).

Heywood's friend, the chaplain of Mary, Wm. Forrest, who shared his interest in music not less than in literature, appears to have escaped, probably as a private chaplain, but there seems to have been in his composition more of the reed than the oak.

The rest of the story of Heywood's life may be found in Professor Bang's article (*Englische Studien*, 1907). Here we learn that Ellis became a Jesuit after Wm. Rastell's death in 1565, that he came to Antwerp in 1573 from England " to treat of affairs ", and that his remarkable knowledge of languages led to his remaining in the college. It will be remembered that in 1556 he had written in Italian and published in Florence his *Il Moro*, which he dedicated to Pole.

His father, now a widower, was living in 1573 at Malines, where Ellis used regularly to visit him, but, as that interfered with his duties, the General of the Order gave quarters in 1576 within the college to " old Heywood ", " ce digne vieillard votre vénére père, avec logement et table séparés ". Heywood's letter to Burleigh, asking that his daughter should be allowed to collect and send his rents, was dated from Malines, 18th April, 1575 (see p. 35), and it is gratifying to learn from a second letter in September that his spirited appeal was met sympathetically (see p. 237).

In 1578 troubles broke out at Antwerp, and the Jesuits sent the old man (*vieillàrd octogenaire*) to Cologne under the care of one of their order, but they found, on their arrival at the gates, that their enemies had secured that he should be refused admission. The College at Antwerp was sacked, and John, Ellis, and all the fathers were sent by water to Malines as prisoners. Here they narrowly escaped assassination at the hands of the Orange party, through the intervention of the Catholic Governor, the Archduke Matthias, and they reached the Catholic stronghold of Louvain on 26th May, 1578.

Wm. Rastell had died in 1565, Dr. Clement and his wife were dead in 1572, Johanna Heywood was dead in 1574, Ellis, the most devoted of sons, died on 2nd October, 1578 (*D.N.B.*), and the old man " with the mad merry wit ", that had " made many mad plays ", seems to have out-lived them all.

Pitseus has preserved his last jest :

De quo inter alia memorabilia illud traditur, quod lethali morbo laborans, cum sua peccata praeterita multum deploraret, et bonus quidam Sacerdos qui consolandi causa illi adfuit, illud solum responderet et identidem repeteret, carnem esse fragilem ; retulit ille, ne tu Deum arguere videris, quod me non fecerit piscem.

(Perhaps only a man who had suffered for his faith would in his last hour have chaffed a confessor who could only talk of the frailty of the flesh for seeming to reproach the Deity for not making his penitent a fish.)

William Rastell. Joyce's eldest brother was bound by the terms of his father's will to secure that the family property in Kent did not fall under the Kentish custom of gavelkind, but should pass by entail to the eldest son or heir in regular succession. John Rastell was apparently called in to draw up the will of Joyce's brother, which closes with a list of witnesses headed " teste me Joanne Rastell sen . . . manu propria . . . et me Willmo Rastell scriptore huius testamenti manu propria ". On 1st April, 1525, therefore, William Rastell at the age of seventeen wrote a fair hand and was working under his father in legal practice ; but it was a curious coincidence that one should meet the future editor of the English works of More in this way. Two years later, in 1527, when the ambassadors of France were entertained by Henry VIII and Wolsey, and John Rastell was engaged to devise the elaborate pageant at Greenwich, described in the State Papers as *The Father of Heaven*, William was again collaborating with his versatile parent. In Guildford's elaborate record of expenses, besides the charges of Hans Holbein and others, we have seen that Rastell's account was set out in great detail, and from it we learn that William was employed in the preparation of the show for forty-six days at a fee of eightpence a day.[1]

Antony Wood says that William Rastell went into residence at Oxford in 1525 and carried away a considerable foundation in logic and philosophy, but no degree. If this be true, we may excuse him the degree, seeing that he was writing a will for his father on 1st April, 1525, and working at a pageant for two months in the early summer of 1527. Meanwhile at Chelsea his cousin, Margaret Roper, had translated Erasmus's *Treatise on the Paternoster* and had it printed, and More had the pretty experience of finding Margaret's printer, Berthelet, accused of publishing a book savouring of heresy.

In 1527 and 1528 it is evident that William Rastell was

[1] See p. 18.

making his presence felt in his father's printing business. So far as the extant copies of John Rastell's law books enable us to form an opinion, his activity as a printer seems to fall into two periods. There is his own magnificent burst of industry between 1513 and 1518, and there is the less heroic but more attractive output of the years 1527–9 when he had the assistance of his son, then approaching his twenty-first year.

Mr. Proctor's Hand List of John Rastell's books makes the division clear, if we assign, as on good evidence we may, many of the undated books to the later period. I do not, of course, suggest that the books of the years 1527–9 were rather his son's than his own. They bear, as a rule, his well-known device, they are printed from his types, and they show the old man himself to have been keenly active about them. What I do suggest is that John Rastell had an excellent collaborator in his apprentice in law, pageantry and printing.

Berthelet's trouble with the Vicar-General over the printing of Margaret Roper's little book on *The Lord's Prayer* belongs to a chapter in the history of the regulation of the printing press with which I deal in another section.[1] Wolsey, whose long reign was drawing to a close, had fought Lutheranism and heresy with the old weapons of the ecclesiastical courts and had not succeeded. These weapons had been adequate in the mediaeval days of manuscript books, but they failed in the new days of printing. Tunstall determined to try other ways of stemming the flow of heresy, and he called More to his assistance, granting him a special licence to read heretical books and pamphlets with a view to controverting their errors. More's first controversial work, *The Dialogue of Heresies*, was written in the year 1528 and at once put into John Rastell's hands, who published it in June 1529, by which time William Rastell was of age and about to set up his own press. More was exacting in his demands on his printer, and the *Dialogue*,

[1] See p. 160.

in spite of the obvious care with which it was set up, has a lengthy list of " fawtes escaped in the printing ". This scrupulousness on More's part is easy to understand, seeing that his work was controversial, and mistakes were an occasion for the enemy. More would welcome the independence of a careful young printer, and he set his nephew to work before September 1529 on what was probably the first book that came from his press, the *Supplication of Souls*. For this, William Rastell used a new fount of beautiful secretary type, and except for some large black-letter types used in his title he carried over none of his father's material. John Rastell had two important works of his own in the press, while William was busy on More's *Supplication*, the *Pastyme of People* and a *New Book of Purgatory*. The latter, like More's book, a reply to Simon Fish's attack on the doctrine of Purgatory, appeared 10th October, 1530. The *Pastyme of People*, which was nearing completion in 1529 and appeared soon afterwards, is connected in an interesting way with William Rastell's second book, Caesar's *Commentaries*, a text and translation, with interpolated notes of much interest, of those portions of the Fourth and Fifth Books that deal with Caesar's invasions of Britain. In the introduction to the *Pastyme* the older Rastell speaks scornfully of the legendary account given by Geoffrey of Monmouth of the dawn of British history, and makes the following statement :

But Ye oldest writyng yt we rede of any auctor is ye boke of ye comentarys of Julius Cesar which indytyd yt work him selfe at ye tyme when he cōqueryd this land and made it subiect to the romayns which was xlviii years before the byrth of Cryst. In the which he took grete dylygīce to dyscrybe the realme in so mych yt he shewyth playnly & truly furst ye form & facion of the lād & ye quantyte thereof how many myle it cōteyneth every way, how ye graate ryvers ren & also he dyscryvyth ye maner & ye use of the people how be it he spekyth nothīg of Brute nor for al the serch that he made he could never come to the knowledge how this lād was furst inhabytyd.

We are not surprised, then, to find that William Rastell's second book has the following title :

Julius Cesars Commentaryes / Newly translatyd owte of latin in to Englysh / as cŏcernyth thys realm of England / sumtyme callyd Brytayne ; whych / is the eldyst hystoryer of all / other that can be found / that ever wrote of / this realm of England / 1530.

This again is an attractive piece of printing. The Latin text is in a neat small roman type, and the translation in the pretty secretary used in the *Supplication of Souls*.

With the Caesar I associate two other undated books of William Rastell's, his translation of Cicero's *De Amicitia*, a book for which I have a particular affection as it rests, handsomely bound, at the British Museum in the same volume as the Caxton Ciceros and the English version of the pretty fiction of *Fulgens and Lucrece* by Bonaccorso of Pistoja which Henry Medwall had turned into an Interlude ; the other book is his edition of Medwall's *Nature*. Of the *De Amicitia* it may be said that its careful workmanship and good paper make it worthy of a place in a volume of Caxton's, whilst its secretary type is quite in keeping with Caxton's bolder work and even shows something of the same form and inspiration. Of Medwall's *Nature* this must be said, that it is entirely fitting that it should owe its preservation to the printer-nephew of More who forty years earlier had known Medwall as a chaplain in Cardinal Morton's household.

In 1531 we find from the colophon to his *Register of the Writs* that William Rastell had quarters in Fleet Street, but he appears at no time to have adopted a sign or to have used a device. Instead of a device we find in his bigger books, after 1530, a dignified title-page with a large arched compartment on columns at the base of which are the initials W.R. It is noteworthy that the law book I have just mentioned was to be bought in St. Paul's Churchyard, presumably at his father's shop, at his own house, and at Robert Redman's at Temple Bar. It is interesting to find that Redman was on these terms with the Rastells, because about this time his name appears on some law books for which John Rastell held the royal privilege. At one time I was inclined to think of him as an intruder—Pynson certainly treated him as one—but perhaps his retort to Pynson, " Si Deus nobiscum, quis contra nos ", was justified.

More's first attack upon heretics, the *Dialogue of Heresies*, had, as we have seen, been printed by John Rastell. In 1531 William printed a handsome second edition in secretary, but for the long and laboursome *Confutation of Tyndale's Answer* he employed a new fount of black letter in which Part I appeared during 1532.

More's Chancellorship was of short duration. He took over the great seal in September 1529 and resigned it on 16th May, 1532, and it was during this period, as we have seen, that William Rastell came of age and showed himself to be a printer worthy of his distinguished uncle whose works he was printing. More wrote of his resignation to Erasmus, emphasizing the gracious protestations of the king in acceding to his retirement, and adding a humorous note of satisfaction that even his adversaries had failed so far to come forth complaining of his injustice. Ill-health had something to do with his decision, but we know, and his adversaries knew, the cause to be deeper seated than that. It was one thing to controvert the heretics whose heresy he heartily hated; it was another to serve in high office a king who was affronting his defence of orthodoxy in act and deed. More's decision was of a piece with his character. Though all for a time went well, he was under no delusion as to his position, and it is of great interest here carefully to observe the dates and sequence of events. He resigned in May 1532; in September William Rastell was specially admitted at Lincoln's Inn, More's own Inn, and on the following New Year's Day More's friend Heywood gave to the King a New Year's gift and received one from the King himself. So far the skies had not fallen.[1] The atmo-

---

[1] See p. 44 : " To Heywood . . . item a gilte cup ".

sphere at Court was evidently not unfavourable to More at the beginning of 1533, and there is evidence that during the following twelve months More was fairly free from anxiety, and that both he and William Rastell were hard at work; indeed, the year 1533 was much the most productive year in Rastell's career as a printer. He continued to work at his uncle's *Confutation of Tyndale's Answer*; he printed his *Apology*, his *Letter against John Frith*, his *Debellation of Salem and Bizance*, and his *Answer to (Tyndale's) Poysoned Book*. This last book Rastell finished just before Christmas 1533, but dated 1534, and this seemingly slight inaccuracy was seized upon by adversaries to support an allegation that the book was an attack upon the new *Book of the Articles devised by the King's Council*. More disclaimed this and explained what had occurred. William Rastell had anticipated the New Year by a few days, treating it as beginning on 1st January.

Besides his printing for More, Rastell printed in 1533 Fabyan's *Chronicles* in full. This he may have done by arrangement with the Fabyans, whose arms occupy the full-page verso of the title-leaf. Robert Fabyan was, of course, dead, but there was a John Fabyan, a physician of wealth and literary tastes, living in the parish of St. Clement Danes at this time, who left his English books on medicine and his English *Chronicles* to Lady Marny in 1541. Whether or not it was he who suggested the new edition, it is obvious that John Rastell's very original adaptation of Fabyan, the *Pastyme of People*, had not taken its place. William Rastell's second edition perhaps made amends for his father's rather bold and free abbreviation of the Pynson Fabyan.

Another interesting work of this crowded year, 1533, deserves mention : young John More's translation of the report by the Portuguese, Damyan Goes, to his friend the Archbishop of Upsala, of the church and commonwealth of Prester John. It is an important little book with an innocently pleasant preface by John More to the reader, the

black-letter Heywood plays at the end of the same year. If it should be asked what a protégé of More's was doing to print plays in the beginning of 1533 which make such free sport of curates, priests, pardoners and friars, I would reply that More himself has a pretty answer to the objection in a passage addressed to Tyndale in this same year. Tyndale had tried to score a point by suggesting that More's " derling ", Erasmus, in a book written in More's house, *The Praise of Folly*, had written more than freely of saints and relics and images. " That Boke of Moriae," says More, " dothe indeede but iest uppon the abuses of such thinges after the manner of the disours part in a playe."

William Rastell's printing ceased when More's troubles began. He had printed his books from a house without a sign in St. Bride's Churchyard, Fleet Street, and I had expected to find his name in the Subsidy Roll for St. Bride's parish in 1534. What I found there, however, was that John Heywood had a large house in St. Bride's parish with the high assessment of £40, but that William Rastell's name did not occur. It is not unlikely that he had quarters in Heywood's premises, and that the two were under the same roof when the four plays were printed.

The irritating charge against William Rastell and More in the matter of the New Year's dating of 1534 was followed up in February by the charge against More of holding communication with the nun of Kent, and when he had at length cleared himself of that, there followed the charge to take the Oath of Supremacy. On 17th April, 1534, More went to the Tower, and William Rastell, dropping the now dangerous craft of printing, devoted himself to the study of law. He was joined at Lincoln's Inn on 25th July, 1534, by John Heywood's brother Richard, who was present a year later as a law-clerk at More's trial and is mentioned by Roper as one of his authorities for the account he gives of the proceedings. William Roper and Richard Heywood were close friends and lifelong associates. They became legal partners in the office of Prothonotary of the King's

Bench and shared quarters in Lincoln's Inn. In this year, 1534, of More's imprisonment, and Richard Heywood's admission to Lincoln's Inn, John Heywood was playing the game by cheering the seventeen-year-old daughter of the superseded Queen Katherine.[1]

On the other hand, old John Rastell, as we have seen, had been won over to the side of the Protestants by the young scholar of Christ Church, the martyr John Frith, a charming, witty, and lovable enthusiast. In re-reading one of Rastell's law-suits I came across an unrecorded fragment of a lost book by Rastell on the dorso of a sheet of depositions. It is all that remains of Rastell's second reply to Frith. It is headed *The cause why that Rastell made his boke of purgatory without aleggyng any textes of holy scripture*, and it opens with the phrase : *I marvell gretely that my broder Fryth does hold this. . . .* Frith's reply is still extant, but this fragment is all that exists of Rastell's treatise.[2] (See Appendix VI.)

The story of his estrangement from the More circle and his unfortunate end has been told. More does not mention him in any of the letters and treatises that he wrote in his confinement. " A good man and a very properly lerned man," one of his friends called him, but his ill-balanced enthusiasm and pervicacity were at length laughed at, and he died in prison neglected, caught in the web of the spider, if he is the Fly and Cranmer the Spider of John Heywood's *Spider and the Flie.*[3] Rastell's alienation from his own people is marked by the completion in July 1534 of the conveyance of the family property in Warwickshire to the Wygstons of Leicester.

The imprisonment of More began on Friday, 17th April, 1534, and he remained in a confinement that grew closer as time passed. He was executed on Tuesday, 6th July, 1535, fifteen months later. It is probably to the piety of his

[1] See p. 54.

[2] The depositions and the fragment belong to the law-suit on Theatrical Costumes published by Mr. A. W. Pollard and Mr. H. R. Plomer in *An English Garner* (R.O. Court of Requests, Bundle 8, No. 14). See also p. 220 ff.

[3] See pp. 34 and 209–10.

daughter, Margaret Roper, that we owe in the first instance the preservation of the writings and letters that belong to this period. Cresacre More tells us that she was imprisoned after her father's death and "was threatened very sore because . . . she meant to set her father's works in print". Of these last works of More it is not easy to speak as one feels. Their cheerful courage, strong conviction and genuine simplicity are as impressive as their freshness and ready wit. "Farewell my deare childe," he wrote to Margaret on the day before he died, "and pray for me and I shall for you and all your friends that we may merely (merrily) meet in heaven." Seriousness in More was not sadness. He would have loved George Herbert for his wit not less than for his saintly life. It is doubtful if, when More's English works find a second editor, the controversial works will please many readers, but they are too full of good things to remain out of our reach. The works of the imprisonment, however, are not controversial, and they are a great achievement. In one of the Holbein groups of the More family is shown a Boethius, a favourite book with the household. More's *Comfort against Tribulation* is his own *Consolations of Philosophy*. I sometimes wonder why it is not better known in English homes. It is a cheerful book, not without the interest of playful reminiscence. More's heaven is a place of laughter and mirth. They that sow in tears "shall have in heaven a merye laughing harvest for ever". *Comfort against Tribulation* was, as we shall see, the only work written in prison to be printed before the great volume of the English works appeared, but it had to wait for the accession of Mary.

A year after John Rastell's death in prison, in 1536, his widow, More's sister Elizabeth, died. She appears to have found an asylum in John Heywood's house with her daughter Joan, to whom she left "her ring of gold with the great red stone" and all her personal belongings. Her son William was her executor. More's other sister, Joan Staverton, who lived in widowhood from 1538 to 1542, appointed John

Heywood her executor and left her best bed to William
Rastell, who two years later married Winifred, the young
daughter of Dr. John Clement. It is not without significance
that More's widowed sisters placed their last trust in the
keeping of John Heywood and William Rastell.[1]

More had married his children prudently. The Ropers,
Herons, Danceys, Allingtons and Cresacres were all wealthy,
and More did not involve anyone but himself in his own
deliberate act of conscience. Yet he appears from one of
his last letters to his old friend, Antony Bonvyse, the wealthy
Italian financier of Crosby Hall, to be expressing gratitude
for something more than their old intimacy and Bonvyse's
many generosities. It would seem as if the old Italian had
set More's mind at rest as to the security of his disciples, if
not in England, then abroad.

William Rastell was called to the Bar in the Trinity Term
of 1539, and he prospered. He was now thirty-one. He had
already at the age of twenty-six closed his career as a printer,
and in that craft he had done really distinguished work.
He had also already edited by that time an important law
book for the gentlemen students of the law, and had prefaced
it with a dignified and business-like preface. His work had
marked him out as a young man of character, great industry,
cultivated tastes and unusual ability. He had an orderly
mind, the inflexible will of all the Mores, and their singular
loyalty in friendship. And now he prospered. As evidence
of this we have the records of his purchases of land in 1542,
when for £80 he acquired property of over 100 acres in North
Mymms, in Hertfordshire, and for £200 messuages and land
at Tottenham, the latter interestingly enough from John
Heywood and his son-in-law, Christopher Stubbes. Heywood himself too had prospered, as this property indicates,
and it was probably Heywood's purchase in 1540 of land
in North Mymms that led William Rastell to buy an estate

---

[1] It should be noted that William Rastell's elder brother John had
probably not returned from the Labrador voyage at the time of his mother's
death.

there. Two years later William Rastell married Winifred Clement, the daughter of More's most brilliant disciple,[1] and it was probably William Rastell's new preoccupation in life that kept him out of the trouble that John Heywood, William Roper, John More, Bishop Gardiner's nephew and the parish priest of Chelsea, with others, fell into in 1543. The story of the plot against Cranmer has been told.[2] It was in the year 1544, and under the strain of these anxieties, that More's daughter, Margaret Roper, died and was buried at Canterbury in the Roper's church of St. Dunstan's. How closely the friends of More were concerned in these troubles is indicated by the fact that among those executed was More's parish priest, John Larke, Rector of Chelsea.

William Rastell appears not to have been involved in those things, partly, I think, because of his impending marriage, and partly because he was much absorbed as a young barrister in his new responsibilities. He was called to the Bar, as we have seen, in May 1539. In 1541 he is mentioned in the Black Books of Lincoln's Inn as having clerks under him, and his clerks are again mentioned in 1544, the year of Heywood's troubles, as paying 18d. a week for their commons, " so that they exercise the larnyngs both wt-in that house and wt-out ". In 1545 he was promoted to the office of Pensioner of the Inn.

In 1546 he was Autumn Reader and became a Bencher. He was proceeding rapidly through the stages of promotion in the hierarchy of his Inn. In 1547 he was nominated to examine certain members who had failed in their duties as custodians of the Council Chamber and Library at the Sergeant's Feast, when some one "spoyled [3] the meate ". He was, in fact, one of the busiest and most respected Benchers, and as such took a leading part in the festivities at Westminster at the coronation of "the most worthy and *indolent* Prynce and King ", Edward VI. In 1548 he was Keeper of the Black Book, from which these facts are taken, and in 1549 he was elected, in the third year of the

---

[1] See Pitseus.　　　[2] See p. 63.　　　[3] I.e. stole.

reign, Treasurer of the Inn. Then on 2nd February, 1549–50, occurs the startling entry, " Rastell the Treasurer fined £10 because he went to foreign parts without leave of the Governors ". He had revolted against the Protestant rigours of Edward's advisers. An Inquisition held at the Guildhall on 27th February, 1550–1, a year later, states that he " deceitfully and rebelliously " took flight to Louvain on 21st December, 1549, with his wife and her parents, and that his goods and chattels were forfeit to the King. He is shown as the owner of a lease of a valuable messuage named Skales Inn in Whittington College and seven other messuages in the City. His household goods, including seventy yards of hangings, were assessed at a high value, and this Middlesex Inquisition took no cognizance of his Hertfordshire property. Rastell had been preceded in his flight by Antony Bonvyse. For the first three years of Edward's reign London Catholics had been protected by Bishop Bonner, and it was his deposition that led Bonvyse, the Rastells and the Clements to seek a foreign sanctuary. Bonner was accused of allowing Masses to be said in private houses, and generally of failing to carry out the repressive measures of the Reformers.[1]

William Rastell was an exile for three and a half years, and during that time he occupied himself in compiling and preparing for the press More's English works and the important law books that Tottell printed afterwards. In the preface to the most important of the law books, *The Collection of Entrees*, he writes: " This book, which (with such copies as I had, being out of England and lacking conference with learned men) to the furtherance of the practice of the law, I have finished the eight and twenty day of Marche, in the yeare of our Lord God a thousand five hundred three score and four ". An equally important work, *The Collection of the Statutes*, probably also occupied him, and there is good reason for supposing that he translated his father's *Expositiones terminorum legum*. But a

[1] See *John Clement and his Books* by A. W. R., *The Library*, March 1926.

cruel blow fell upon him before his exile was over. Four days after the death of Edward VI, and before Mary was proclaimed, his wife Winifred died of fever in Louvain and was buried in St. Peter's Church, aged twenty-six; [1] and having laid his wife to rest, William Rastell returned to England with his co-exiles, her parents, John and Margaret Clement, and the Bonvyses. Winifred Rastell's epitaph may be read in Pitseus: "Latinae linguae non imperita, Graecam vero eximie callens, sed moribus et vitae sanctimonia nemini postponienda. Cui (pie lector) Deum quaeso, deprecare propitium". In November Richard Tottel printed More's *Comfort against Tribulation*.

We next hear of William Rastell from the Black Book of Lincoln's Inn. On Ascension Day, 1554, it was reported at a meeting of the Governors:

In this Easter time anno primo Mariae reginae Mr William Rastell one of the Benchers of this house of Lincoln's Inn gave towards the furnishing of the altar in the Chapel in the Howse, a greate image or picture in a table of the taking down of Cryste from the Cross and two curtains of green and yellow sarcenet for to hang at the ends of the same altar and also a cloth of green and yellow sarcenet lined with canvas to hang before the said altar : which things the said Mr Rastell gave to have the prayers hereunder written for the souls hereunder specified.[2] Wherfore at the request of the said Mr Rastell it is at this present council granted and agreed by the whole consent of all the Masters of the Bench of Lincoln's Inn present at this council that at all times hereafter every priest that shall serve in the Chapel shall in every of his Masses that he shall say at the said altar say at the beginning of the Mass before the Epistle and in the end of the Masse, a "collett" for the sowles of Winifred Rastell wyff to the said William and of all the parents kinfolk and friends ; and also shall in every of the said Masses remember the same souls in the memento pro mortuis. Also the said Mr Rastell did then at his costs for his said wife's soul gild the "V knoppys" of the canope for the sacrament whch cost him 11 1s.

[1] Pitseus states that she died 17th July, 1553, and had been married nine years.

[2] Most unfortunately no names are given in the Black Book. I have been permitted to examine it at Lincoln's Inn.

Margin. Hic ordo propter stolidam abhominaconem et superstitionem abolitur ad Consilium tentum 16 Aug., anno regni Dominae Reginae Elizabethae 23° (1581).

The next entry in the Black Book is the last. It is to record the presentation of the accounts of William Rastell (now) Serjeant-at-Law, the Treasurer, and it refers to the customary gift made by the Inn to the new Serjeants.

We have already referred to Cresacre More's statement that Margaret Roper had contemplated the publication of her father's works. After her death William Rastell had taken over this pious office and carried the works as far as he had then collected them to Louvain. Lest, he tells us in his preface to the English *Works*, they should in time perish, unless they were collected together and printed in one whole volume.

I did diligently collect and gather together as many of those his works, books, letters and other writings printed and unprinted in the English tongue, as I could come by, and the same, certain years in the evil world passed, *keeping in my hands very surely and safely* now lately have caused to be imprinted in this one volume.

We have seen that he had the *Comfort against Tribulation* printed by Tottel at once on his return in November 1553. His preface to the *Works* is dated 30th April, 1557, four years later, and addressed to Queen Mary. I will not speak at length on Rastell's editorial care, the value of the marginal notes, particularly of those explaining the intimate family references in the last letters, nor his attention to accuracy of sequence. William Rastell's work is a monument of loyal care. But I am so bold as to be thankful that at the last moment he added to the 1,428 pages that begin with the life of Mirandula fourteen pages of verse written by Mayster Thomas More in his youth for his pastime,[1] so that the great volume opens with " A mery

[1] There is no doubt that these fourteen pages were added. They are paged independently and belong to the introductory leaves.

jest how a *sergeant* would learne to playe the frere ". This argues a sense of fun in Mr. Sergeant Rastell.

Under Queen Mary, William Rastell more than recovered his material prosperity. On 25th October, 1558, he was raised to the Bench, and it is interesting to note that Jasper Heywood was appointed Lord of Misrule at Lincoln's Inn for the Christmas revels of the same year. Young Heywood had already probably finished his translation of the first of his three Senecan tragedies, the *Troas* which Tottel printed in 1559. I know of no better illustration of the rapid advance of Renaissance thought and feeling than the fact that John Heywood's *Spider and the Flie* and his son's *Troas* were only separated by three years. By walking warily in the troubled days of Edward VI, John Heywood had secured for his sons an uninterrupted and sound education, and Jasper succeeded Ellis as a Fellow of All Souls. Nothing in the story of the More circle is more strangely impressive than the manner in which the rings of loyalty widened in succeeding generations. That John Heywood and his old wife Joan, William Rastell and his wife's parents, Dr. John Clement and Margaret Giggs, should renounce their prosperity and again become exiles we can understand ; they were More's *discipuli familiarissimi*. But before the parents fled from the Elizabethan rigour, Ellis and Jasper Heywood were in Rome. Jasper had become a Jesuit, and Ellis had written his *Il Moro*. In view of his family history one can appreciate the spiritual struggle that John Heywood's grandson passed through ; I refer to John Donne, Dean of St. Paul's. The first years of Elizabeth's reign had passed before William Rastell and the Clements again fled —from Gravesend—to Louvain on 3rd January, 1562–3, John Heywood and his wife followed on 20th July, 1564, and none of them returned. The flight of a Justice of the Queen's Bench to the protection of a foreign sovereign, without licence, was a grave misdemeanour, and a special Commission (anno 4) sat at the Guildhall in October to take an inventory of his belongings, which became forfeit to

the Crown. The inquest assessed the value of the personal
belongings left in his chambers at Sergeant's Inn where
apparently he had lived. The findings began with a list
of some forty odd books, of which half are law books. The
rest include a Euclid, a Eusebius, a St. Augustine, an
(Erasmus) New Testament in Latin and Greek, a Horace
with commentary, a Psalter in Greek, Eliot's Dictionary,
an *Aeneid* in French, a Greek Dictionary, a Cicero *de Oratore*,
a French Testament, Gardiner's book against Bucer, Euripides in Latin and Greek, an *Illucidarius poeticus*, *Adrianus
de modo Latinae loquendae*, a Bible in parchment, Lucian's
Dialogues in Greek, and a Theodore Gasius. The prices
named vary from 4s. for a book of Statutes from Henry III
to Henry VIII, to 4d. for the *Olde Abridgment* of the Statutes.
The MS. Bible on parchment was valued at 2s. ; Eliot's
Dictionary, the Euripides and the French Virgil were
priced at 1s. each. The *Grand Abridgment*, which John
Rastell priced new at 42s., was valued at 3s. 4d.

Like Chaucer's Sergeant of the Law, William Rastell
had many robes. His gowns violet and scarlet, and cloaks
faced with fur, sarcenet, velvet, sable or martin varied in
value from £6 13s. 4d. to 30s. His gowns and caps are
valued in all at over £30. Then there was the furniture,
the beds, hangings, the maps, a bow and a sheaf of arrows
(2s. 6d.), and a corselet with all parts (13s. 4d.), and finally
a *bone wrapped in a canvas* (2d.). These things Rastell
left behind him in his chambers in Sergeant's Inn, and they
probably represent what he was content to leave rather
than all he had to leave. As compared with the books,
maps were highly priced, a French map and Italian map
and a "universal" map were valued at 12s. Relative
values may be assessed by the price (2s. 6d.) of a long seat
described as a side form. This was probably a substantial
oak form such as we might nowadays pick up for 30s. in
the country. William Rastell did not long survive his
second exile. He died of a fever on 27th August, 1565,
and was buried beside his wife in St. Peter's Church at

Louvain. Men of law are not always punctilious in their attention to their wills, but nothing could exceed the care and skill with which William Rastell negotiated this difficult business. He filed an autograph duplicate copy with the registrar at Antwerp, and had it attested in his own presence on 8th August, 1564. Probate was granted to Dr. Clement and Ellis Heywood on 5th October, 1565. Ellis he made his heir, leaving him the rents, which he continued to draw while he lived, of William Rastell's lands and houses in North Mymms.

He had, however, purchased from the City of Antwerp a perpetual annuity of 780 florins which he left partly to Ellis Heywood, partly to Bartholomew More, provided that he did not cease to be an exile so long as England was Protestant, and partly to charitable uses. His gold locket with the portrait of More, all his printed books except law books, all his wearing apparel, he left to Ellis Heywood, and he left rings and jewels to all his relatives and friends, including his brother John who received a gold ring with astronomical figures that remind us of his father. I have told the story of the remaining years of Rastell's survivors in exile and how old John Heywood outlived them all to make upon his deathbed a last merry jest. And now, as I draw towards the close of my chapter, I would suggest that it is right to give to William Rastell's edition of the *English Works of Sir Thomas More* the place of honour among his many achievements. More's influence dominated and directed the life and fortunes of his nephews, Rastell and Heywood, and it has seemed to me worth while to gather together the story of their relationship, not only because it makes a coherent and inspiring tale, but also because it helps us to feel ourselves something of More's influence.

There is one small matter on which I would add a word. By the courtesy of the Library Committee and the Librarian of Lincoln's Inn, I was permitted to examine the books and manuscripts, bequeathed to the Inn by Sir Ranulph Cholmeley in 1563, the year before Rastell left England.

Four of these books had been the property of William Rastell, and in one of them is written the note :

Memorandum that I William Rastell the xvi day of March in the xxx year of kyng Henry the VIII have sold to Randall Cholmeley my fyve gret bokes of yeres wherof this is one for the some of xxxviiiis.viiid. which the same day he hath payd me.

Each of these volumes has his name in neat Greek characters, and many of the manuscript notes are of interest, as, for example, the reference to William Rastell's reading in 1548 on the Statute *Quia Emptores*. Together they form a most valuable collection of early printed Year Books, the work of Pynson, Robert Redman, Wyer and Berthelet.[1]

[1] The colophons of Berthelet show high spirits. His *Year Book* of 14 Henry VII he hopes will tickle the most delicate palate, and concludes :

Scio per Jovem non omnino displiciturum hunc libellum.

It is a pretty piece of work in secretary dated 1529.

CHAPTER IV

THE BEGINNINGS OF THE ENGLISH SECULAR AND ROMANTIC DRAMA (I)

STUDENTS of the early Tudor drama are familiar with the fact that the most interesting and original plays printed during the reign of Henry VIII came from the presses of John and William Rastell. This bibliographical fact has much significance in the story of the origins of the Tudor drama, and the investigation of the circumstances that lie behind it opens the way to conclusions of some importance for the historians of literature.

An attempt has been made in recent years entirely to restate the problem of the early Tudor drama by Dr. C. W. Wallace, whose *Evolution of the English Drama* postulates, curiously, not evolution, but a " square break ". Dr. Wallace finds in the literary musician, William Cornyshe, the great originator. He claims that Cornyshe is the author of *The Four PP.*, *The Pardonere and Frere* and *Johan Johan*, a trilogy of plays traditionally assigned to John Heywood. He claims further that Cornyshe was the only dramatist living who had " opportunity, impetus, or skill " to write in the new manner three other plays, *Gentleness and Nobility*, *The Four Elements*, and *Calisto and Meliboea*. If we add to this list of plays, assigned by Dr. Wallace to Cornyshe, Heywood's three unchallenged plays, Medwall's *Nature*, and his newly discovered *Fulgens and Lucres*, we have all of the plays of which I shall have to speak ; and it should be remarked that ten of the eleven were printed by the

94

Rastells, whilst it has been suggested by Professor A. W. Pollard as probable that there was a Rastell edition, now lost, of the eleventh, *The Four PP.*

Cornyshe, who is called by his protestant the octavian Shakespeare, was master of the boys of the Chapel Royal during the earlier years of the reign of Henry VIII. He is prominent in the Revels Accounts of the early years of the sixteenth century, but his place in history lies in the story, not of the popular drama, but of that extravagant medley of music, pageantry and dance, the Court masque. The attribution of six plays to a definite dramatist on the sole ground that he alone of all Englishmen then living was capable of writing them is not likely, I think, to secure a good foundation for a study of the evolution of the drama. " No other dramatist," Dr. Wallace says, " but the impossible Medwall was then writing."

It is " the impossible Medwall ", however, who has now to be put in the place of honour at the head of the line of Tudor dramatists. In dismissing Medwall to make room for Cornyshe, Dr. Wallace was apparently misled by Payne Collier, whose very circumstantial and graphic illustration of Medwall's dullness he accepted without, it seems, examining the document at the Record Office in which it was said to be found. The anecdote which occurs in Collier's *History of Dramatic Poetry* (p. 69) gives an account, now widely circulated, of the failure of a lost play of Medwall, called, not without irony, *The Fyndyng of Troth.*

Quoting from a Chapter House Roll of Revels Accounts, Collier shows items for costumes for Venus, Beauty, a Fool, and ladies and gentlemen who took parts in the entertainments at Richmond in 1513. These entries, correctly transcribed by Collier, are to be found at the Record Office in a large bound volume, which bears on each leaf the punctures of roll stitching (Misc. Bks., Exch., T.R., 217). But according to Collier, there was " a singular paper folded up in the roll," giving an account of two interludes performed on this occasion, one by William Cornyshe entitled, *The*

Tryumpe of Love and Beauty, in which Venus and Beauty took part ; the other, Medwall's *Fyndyng of Troth.* After a eulogistic description of Cornyshe's allegorical device, Collier quotes from the " singular paper " the following note on Medwall's play, concluding with a facsimile of Cornyshe's signature :

Inglyshe and the oothers of the Kynges pleyers after pleyed an Interluyt whiche was wryten by Mayster Medwall but yt was so long yt was not lyked : yt was the fyndyng of Troth who was carried away by ygnoraunce and yprocesy. The foolys part was the best, but the kyng departyed befor the end to hys chambre.

There is no trace of this paper in the bound volume, nor is anything known of it at the Record Office, where the documents for this period have been recently subjected to a close scrutiny for the revision of the first volume of the *Letters and Papers of Henry VIII.* As it could not have any bearing on the business of receipts and payments of which the roll was a record, its insertion does not find a ready explanation. I would suggest, therefore, that it is wise to treat the story of the folded paper with suspicion.

It is, however, upon this story, with its implied contrast between Cornyshe of the new school and Medwall of the old, that Dr. Wallace has rested his thesis ; and unhappily his only reference to the folded paper is under the phrase, " a well-known document ".

The wrong done to Medwall has been righted by time. Readers of *The Times Literary Supplement* may recall the signed article by Dr. F. S. Boas on 20th February, 1919, on the Mostyn Plays then awaiting sale by auction at Sothebys. Henry Medwall's play of *Fulgens and Lucres* had come to light. It was sold a month later to go to America for £3,400, a figure that does not exaggerate its importance.[1]

---

[1] With great public spirit, Mr. Henry E. Huntington, its new owner, has published a photographic facsimile of the play with an introductory note by Mr. Seymour de Ricci.

Halliwell-Phillipps was right, after all, when he added to the fifth edition of his *Outlines* in 1885 the note :

The most ancient English drama which is known to exist was written about the year 1490 by the Rev. Henry Medwall, chaplain to Morton, Archbishop of Canterbury, and afterwards printed by Rastell.

The play is one of remarkable interest historically, how interesting may appear from the following account of the source of its plot and the nature of its structure.

A fragment of the play, two leaves in the Bagford collection at the British Museum, was reproduced in facsimile by Dr. R. B. McKerrow, in Bang's *Materialien zur Kunde des älteren Englischen Dramas*, vol. xii (Louvain, 1905), and later was printed with a foreword by Dr. W. W. Greg in the *Collections* of the Malone Society, 1908. In 1911 Professor Czeizenach announced in the Shakespeare *Jahrbuch* that the source of the plot was apparently to be found in the *De Vera Nobilitate* of Bonaccorso of Pistoja, which he had come across in a summarized form. Independent investigation has confirmed Czeizenach's note.

Bonaccorso was an Italian humanist, a learned lawyer, a Petrarchan enthusiast, and writer of Ciceronian Latin, as well as of vernacular poetry. He held magisterial office in Florence, enjoyed the patronage of Carlo Malatesta, Lord of Rimini, to whom he dedicated his *De Vera Nobilitate*, and died in 1429, in the same year as his patron.[1]

The subject of Bonaccorso's *débat* will become clear as we proceed. But it may be explained that the story is a pseudo-realistic romance of Roman life written in the artificial style of a rhetorical exercise in Ciceronian Latin.

Medwall's immediate source was not, however, the Latin of the Italian humanist, but an English version printed by Caxton in 1481, translated by John Tiptoft, Earl of Worcester, from a French version, the work of Jean Mielot, secretary and translator to Philip of Burgundy, printed

[1] An admirable account of Bonaccorso is given by G. Zaccagnini in his *Studi de Litteratura Italiana*, vol. i, 1899.

H

by Colard Mansion of Bruges, Caxton's collaborator. This Caxton version of Bonaccorso's story of *Fulgens and Lucres* I accidentally discovered while examining a Caxton Cicero in 1917 at the Museum. The discovery gave an added interest to the announcement of the sale of the lost play, *Fulgens and Lucres*, and I availed myself of the sale-room privilege of turning over the pages of the little quarto.

The Caxton version of *De Vera Nobilitate* occurs in a volume containing Cicero's *Friendship* and *Old Age*, and it is connected with these by its introduction, the three pieces making up Caxton's book. It opens with the words :

Here followeth the Argument of the declamation which laboureth to shewe wherein honoure shoulde reste :

Whan thempyre of Rome moste floured . . .

From this argument we learn that Fulgens, a noble senator of Rome, had a daughter, Lucresse, of " marveyllous beaute ", " grete attemperaunce of lyf ", " worshipful conduyt of manners ", " grete force of wysdom ", and " plenteous understanding of lectrure ". Lucresse had two wooers, Publius Cornelius, a descendant of the Scipios, of wealth and following, whose " grete studye rested in huntyng, hauking, syngyng and disporte ", and Gayus Flaminius, " borne of lower stocke " of moderate riches and virtuous manners, whose " grete studye was . . . to helpe his frende and contrey ", but who in time of peace was " right busye and laboryous in his bokes ". Lucresse submits the decision to her father, who refers it to the senate, before whom the lovers make their declamations at length.

In the Interlude this argument is summarized in an account given by A to B of the " substaunce " of the play, the account beginning almost in the words of Caxton :

When thempire of Rome was in such flour.

It was too much for the little fellowship of players of interludes to present the Senate in session, so Medwall makes the lovers put their cases to Lucresse. This occupies the greater part of Part II and is solemnly done in rime royal, a distinction reserved for the Roman element in the play ; the humours of A and B, on the other hand, are maintained in rime doggerel. Medwall is bold enough to declare for virtuous poverty and gives the prize to Gayus Flaminius, whereas Caxton follows the tradition of the *débat* by leaving the verdict open :

As touchyng the sentence dyffynytyf gyven by the Senate . . . I fynd none as yet pronounced . . . Thene I wolde demaunde of theym that shall rede or here the book whiche of this tweyne was moost noble . . . and to him juge ye this noble & vertuous lady Lucresse to be maryed.

Bonaccorso had to consider the feelings of a Malatesta, Mielot of a Burgundy, and Caxton of a " most dread souerayn ". It was therefore a happy stroke of Medwall's to give the woman's verdict, a privileged decision, excusable if questioned on a plea of natural affection ; it was not the finding of the " faders conscript ". To compromise on final issues is the wisdom of old men ; it is not the way of women. There is something Portia-like in the assurance and competence of Lucres.

We must now turn to the lighter side of Medwall's comedy, the humours of the two boys, A and B, and it is probable that in spite of the interest of the main plot, the humorous underplot in " rime doggerel " will prove to be of the higher importance. Two boys, A and B, have " well eaten " at the Cardinal's banquet when B tells A that a play is about to be performed. There is nothing in the world that A loves as much as a play :

I trow your owyn selfe be oon (he says) of them that shall play. Nay (says B) I am none.

But B, who knows the plot, narrates it to A. The principal actors enter. A takes service with Gayus Flaminius, and B with his rival ; and whilst the masters debate their claims to the hand of the mistress, the boys make sport for the lookers-on by wooing her maid.

He was ordained acolyte [1] in April 1490, and described as of the diocese of Winchester, a term of wide signification, seeing that it included Southwark, which adjoins Lambeth. Two years later, by patent dated 27th August, 1492, he was presented by the Crown to the Rectory of Balynghem, in the marches of Calais, and was instituted on the following day by the Archbishop.[2]   A further evidence of Court favour appears in a royal grant by patent on 17th September, 1493, of the Rectory of Newton, in the diocese of Norwich, but for some reason unknown he did not take up the living. He is described in Morton's Register (f. 169) as *Capellanus*, the description being amplified on the title-pages of his plays by the Rastells, who describe him as " late chapelayne to ye ryght reverent fader in god Johan Morton cardynall and Archbysshop of Caunterbury ".[3] As there is no evidence that he proceeded farther in holy orders than the degree or order of acolyte, we must assume that he remained virtually a layman, which is perhaps what Pitseus implies by the term *sacerdos saecularis*. A Chancery suit in which Medwall was defendant, discovered by Mr. H. R. Plomer, who has communicated it to me, throws an interesting light on the nature of Medwall's activities as one of Morton's chaplains, and indicates one of the ways in which he was rewarded for his services. The immense machinery, both provincial and diocesan, over which Morton presided gave him the patronage of many offices of a semi-legal character. There was the great Prerogative Court, the Court of Arches, the Commissary Courts of Canterbury and of Calais, the Deaneries of Croydon, Shoreham and Bocking, and a number of other Peculiar Courts. These were served by a semi-clerical army of registrars, commissaries, recorders, scribes, apparitors and " fermours " ; and it appears from Mr. Plomer's suit that muniments, books and records of, it may be, one or more of these courts were, at the time of Morton's

---

[1] Lambeth Library : Register, *Morton*, f. 140.

[2] Register, *Morton*, f. 153.

[3] *Erat autem archiepiscopo Joanni Mortono à sacellis atque consuetudine domestica* [Bale].

death, in the hands of Henry Medwall, who refused to deliver
them up to Thomas Goldstone,[1] who, as Prior of Christ
Church, Canterbury, assumed, *sede vacante*, all " ordinarie
and spirituelle jurisdicion within the provynce ". Morton
died 12th October, 1500, and his successor, Henry Dean,
did not assume office until 22nd July, 1501. The interval
was unusually long, for Thomas Langton, elected to the
See on 22nd January, 1500–1, died five days later of the
plague. As Dean had taken over the Great Seal on Morton's
death, it was he who, early in February, heard Goldstone's
suit against Medwall. Whatever the result of the suit,
Medwall scored a triumph of sorts, for on 27th February
Letters of Protection of a remarkably comprehensive character were granted to him by letters patent issued by
Dean under the great seal, which nullified the Prior's attack
and rendered Medwall, his servants and deputies free from
arrest, distraints, or fines. It is clear that Medwall was
well friended. The Crown had rewarded him by the gift
of livings and Morton had given him offices. Goldstone
tried to deprive him of these, and judging by the number
of administrative offices that he filled during the vacancy
of the See he may have succeeded.[2] Medwall appears to
have resisted him successfully until Langton's sudden death
gave him a second spell of interregnal authority. On 29th
June, 1501, a successor was appointed to his Calais living,[3]
*vacantem per liberam resignationem Domini Henrici Medwall,
capellani, ultimi rectoris*.[4] In the introduction to *Fulgens
and Lucres* (ed. Boas and Reed) I stressed the clause in
Medwall's Letters of Protection extending the " safeguards "
to Calais and beyond the seas—*tam infra dictum regnum
nostrum Angliae quam alia dominia nostra ubicumque consti-*

---

[1] Goldstone was a notable man. He built the famous Christ Church Gate
at Canterbury, and finished the Harry Tower, the final designs for which
had been submitted to Morton. (See *Christ Church Letters*, No. 58, Camden
Soc.) See p. 240 for transcript of the suit *Goldstone* v. *Morton*.

[2] See Register, *Blamyr*, at Somerset House, and Challenor Smith's introduction to P.C.C. Wills, 1383–1558, pp. xv-xix.

[3] P.R.O., Patent Rolls.

[4] Register, *Morton*, f. 169.

tuta—and conjectured that Medwall may have left England. This remains a possibility, but Goldstone's Chancery suit is in itself an adequate explanation of the Letters. He was apparently alive—and it is the last record of him at present known—on 26th July, 1501, when his successor was instituted to the Calais living. As John Rastell, who must have known him—they were both repaying " obligations " to the Treasurer of the King's Household in 1500–1—refers to him with some circumstance as Morton's chaplain, this presumably was the last significant office he held. Bale, his earliest biographer (1548), in stating that he flourished *c.* 1500, may be held to support the view that he did not long survive Morton.

In turning from Medwall to Rastell, the printer of *Fulgens and Lucres*, we must first note that there is every reason to suppose that the two men were known to one another. We have seen that before Morton's death in 1500 John Rastell was a familiar member of the More circle, and one infers from his *Utopia* that Thomas More's intimacy with the household life of the Cardinal was resumed during the years that he and Rastell were reading law in London. The fact that we owe the preservation of the two Medwall plays to the Rastells is therefore not surprising; nor is it strange to find that Rastell's own dramatic work bears obvious marks of the influence of Medwall. His play of the *Four Elements* is very distinctly influenced by Medwall's *Nature*, although it is in no sense a morality. Its aim is to awaken an interest in natural science : it is the work of an enthusiast of a new era, who felt the romantic possibilities of the age of discovery in which he was conscious of living. The stage, like his printing press, was a medium through which he might influence and kindle, or at any rate serve, his generation. His references in the play to his own voyage,[1] and the fact that these are explained in the lawsuit, of which we have already given a brief account, make it clear that there can be no doubt who wrote the play. It

[1] See Appendix I, p. 187 : The Voyage in the year 1517.

is attributed to Rastell by Bale, and any question that may have arisen from the fact that the unique copy of the *Four Elements* is anonymous [1] may now be held to have been removed. But more than this : knowing the play to be his, we may take further evidence and examine his claim to the authorship of the other two plays that he printed.

The *Four Elements* has come down to us in a single copy, which is imperfect. Indeed, if Rastell followed his master Medwall in writing his *Interludes* in two parts,[2] then we have less than half of the original, and this, I think, is more than probable, since Bale describes it as a very long comedy— *longissima comoedia*. Indeed, of the ten " diuers matters ", points of natural philosophy, that are promised in the preface, only the first four are dealt with. The sixth is " of the generation and cause of well-springs and rivers ; and of the cause of hot fumes that come out of the earth ; and of the cause of the baths of water in the earth, which be perpetually hot ". We may gather some notions as to Rastell's views on fumes and hot baths from the passage in the *Pastyme of People* under Bladud, the founder of Bath :

a grete nigromancyer, as the story seyth, and by y^t craft made there ye hote bathys, but other clerkis hold opynyon that they come naturally of ye grounde. . . . Some phylozophers holde that ye cause thereof is thiss : that whan there is a hote fume, etc.

Possibly under the article " Stones ", he worked in views on the composition of the " stones at Stonehenge . . . all of one gryt ", which he gives us under Aurelius Ambrosius. For the most part the *Pastyme* is an abbreviation of Fabyan, but it is enriched at intervals by characteristic asides ; and even the omissions, as I have already suggested, are often illuminating, as when he refrains from repeating that it was for witchcraft that Jeanne d'Arc was burnt.

When we find an aside or critical remark therefore in the *Pastyme* we hear Rastell speaking, and as we know that we are listening to him in the *Four Elements*, we are prepared

[1] The only extant copy, being incomplete, has no colophon.
[2] *Gentleness and Nobility* is in two parts.

for coincidences. If we find like coincidences occurring in another play printed by Rastell, *Gentleness and Nobility*, of which he said in the colophon, " Johēs rastell me fieri fecit ", we may consider that the question of the authorship of this play too is opening to proof. Before we go farther, however, it should be noted that as in the *Four Elements* one feels the influence of Medwall's *Nature*, so in *Gentleness and Nobility* the theme of Medwall's *Fulgens and Lucres*, " wherein honour (or nobility) shall rest ", is the dramatist's subject. The value of the play lies not in its dramatic power, but in the vigour, boldness and character of its author's reasoning. There is no suggestion of romance in the setting ; the Merchant, Gentleman and Ploughman walk on and conduct their controversy without any plot or dramatic device to explain why they are there or why the subject should be in their minds at all. If the debate had any dramatic appropriateness it must have been in the circumstances of the time ; and if, as I believe, it is closely related to the anonymous interlude, *Goodly Queen Hester*, it is a Wolsey play like Skelton's *Magnificence* ; and Skelton's play is assigned to John Rastell's press.

In the first or Roman section of the *Pastyme*, under the article *Publius Valerius Publicola*, Rastell tells us that when a dictator's term of office was completed, he was answerable to complaints alleged against him and punishable for offences. To this he attributes the high standard of Roman law and justice and the growth of Rome in riches and power.

Wold God, he adds, it was so used at this day in the realme of England, that euery jugge and other offycers hauyng auctoryte to execute yᵉ lawis, or to gouern or to rule in any office, shold be remouable at iiij or v yere or lesse and then to answere to all complayntis that shold be allegid agayns him, and to be ponished for euery offence that he had committed in his rome, and then ther wold not be so mich extorcione and oppressione of the pore people, nor so many iniuries as is now a-days.[1]

[1] Written in 1529, this passage may well reflect Rastell's attitude towards Wolsey.

Later, under Edward I, he finds an instance of such an inquest into the conduct of officials :

Many complaints were made of his offycers as mayres, sheryffes, baylyffes, exchetours, and dyuers other. Wherfore he ordayned his justyce to make inquisicyons therof, whiche after was called Trolbaston ; where by forfeytours and fynes, the kynge . . . fylled his coffers agayne.

To this Rastell himself adds the comment :

Nevertheless, this kynge did great good within the realme of Englande, for those offenders were well chastyced, and were moche more meker and better, and the pore cõmons lyued in moche more rest and peace.

The stage, like the printing press, was an instrument to Rastell for the mission he so often speaks of, his work for the " Commonweal ". It is arresting, therefore, to find in the concluding stanzas of *Gentleness and Nobility* the passage that follows :

> But because that men of nature euermore
> Be frayle & folowyng sensualyte
> Yt is impossyble in a maner therfore
> For any gouernours that be in auctoryte
> At all tymys Just & indyfferent to be
> Except they be brydelyd & ther to compellyd
> By some strayt laws for them deuysyd.

> As thus that no man such rome occupye
> But certayn Yerys & than to be remouyd
> Yet that whyle bound to attend dylygently
> And yf he offend & surely prouyd
> wyth out any fauour that he be ponyhysshyed
> for the ponysshment of a Juge or offycer
> Doth more good than of thousand other.

> And untyll that such orders be deuysyd
> Substauncyally / and put in execucyon
> Loke neuer to see the world amended
> Nor of the gret myschefes the reformacion
> But they that be bounde to see the thinges done
> I pray god of his grace put in theyr myndys
> To reforme shortly suche thynges amys.

And though that I myselfe now percase
Thus myn oppynyon haue publyshed
Or any of my felowes here in this place
In any poynt here haue us abused
we beseche you to holde us excused
And so the auctor herof requyreth you all
And thus I comyt you to god eternall
AMEN
Johēs rastell me fieri fecit.

We learn from the article "Henry IV" that the *Pastyme* was compiled in 1529. In this year Rastell produced another work entitled *A Newe Boke of Purgatory*. He nowhere mentions Simon Fish, with whose general position in the *Supplication for Beggars* he certainly had much sympathy, but the *Boke of Purgatory* was written to combat Fish's statement that many men of " greate litterature and iudgment ", for the love that they have " unto the trouth and unto the comen welth . . . declare theyre oppinion . . . that there is no purgatory ", but that it is an invention of the spiritualty.

More replied to Fish in the same year in his *Supplication of Souls*, in which the souls in Purgatory appealed against the isolation that threatened them, and besought their brethren on earth to think what their action involved.

Rastell bases his proof on " natural reason and good philosophy " and conducts his case by dialogue ; Gyngemyn, a Mohammedan Turk, and Comyngo an Almayne, carry the thesis through three books, the " Almayne " playing the part of the listener. It is agreed that no scriptural allusions are to be admitted ; on this point there is much emphasis laid :

But yet one thynge I will warne the, says the Turk, consyderyng that my onely purpose is to proue the thynge (the existence of Purgatory) by reason / that . . . thou aledge no manner text no authoryte neither of the bokys of the olde byble / nor of the newe testament, neyther of no other boke . . . of the deuynite of thy crysten faythe.

We have here a characteristic Rastell attitude. He is the apostle of " natural reason and good philosophy ".

His faith in the appeal of reason is remarkable. Thus in *Gentleness and Nobility*, the Ploughman, who is attacking the laws and custom of inheritance, is met by the knight with the text " tibi dabo terram hanc et semini tuo " : whereon he replies :

> *Ploughman.* Thou answerest me now euen lyke a fole
> As some of these fonde clarkes that go to scole
> when one putteth to them a subtyll questyon
> of phylozophy to be prouyde by reason.
>
> .   .   .   .   .
>
> Then they will aledge some auctoryte
> of the lawes or elles of deuynite
> whiche in no wyse men may denye
> And yet ye knowe well that of phylozophy
> The pryncyples oft contraryant be
> Unto the very grounds of deuynite.

To estimate the value of this coincidence one must remember that we have here a very advanced position for the early Tudor mind. As to its dramatic appropriateness, we may recall that the mediaeval ploughman enjoyed literary privileges.

Rastell's central position as the apostle of " natural reason and good philosophy " is in the warp and weft of the Interlude. The best way to convert the people, he says :

> Ys to perswade them by natural reason
> For when that a man by hys owne reason
> Juggyth hymself for to offend
> That grudgyth his conscyens & gyffeth compuncyon
> Into hys herte to cause hym amend.
>
> *G. and N.*

Or as he says in the *Boke of Purgatory* :

There is nothing in the worlde shall alter and chaunge a mannes mynde and beleue so well and surely / as shall the iugement of hio owne reason.

B. of P., II, Cap. I.

The *Boke of Purgatory* deals with the Existence of God in Book I, the Immortality of Man's Soul in Book II, and

Purgatory in Book III. It is a fascinating book, because it so entirely reflects the singularity of Rastell's mind :

Nobleness (he says in I. 4) is that whyche hath leste nede of foreyne helpe / that is to saye of helpe of any other thynge . . . the cause is more noble than the effect . . . everything that takyth any effect hath nede of the cawse . . . God is the most noble thing that can be.

This appears in the Interlude in the following words of the philosophic ploughman :

Ploughman.　Ys not y^t the noblyst thyng in dede
That of all other thynges hath lest nede
As god which reynith etern in blysse
Is not he the noblest thing y^t is . . .
. . . (because he) nedyth the helpe of no nother thyng
To the helpe of his gloryous beyng
But euery other thyng hath nede of his ayde.

To this, the reply is made that " euerie beest fyssh and other foule " is by this reasoning " more noble of birth than a man " :

For man hath more nede of bodely coueryng
Than they haue for they nede no thinge
The bestes haue herr & also a thik skin
The fissh skalis or shells to kepe theyr bodyes in
The foulis fethers & so eueri thing
Bi nature hath his proper couering
Saue man himself which is born all nakyd
And therfore he shuld be than most wrechyd.

The Ploughman readily grants that " consideryng man's body, a beste is more noble & man more wrechyd ", for man must " dayly labour & swete ", dig, kill beasts for meat, cultivate fruits and herbs for drinks,

Yet this not wythstandyng
Man is most noble of creatures lyuyng
Not by hys body for that is impotent
But by his soule beyng so excellent
For by reason of his soule intellectyue
He subdewyth all other bestis that be
By hys wit to releue his necessyte.

Now this line of thought occurs also in the section of the *Boke of Purgatory* that deals with the immortality of man's soul. After distinguishing souls vegetative (plant-life), souls sensitive (animal life), and souls intellective, Gyngemyn, the Turk, replies to Comyngo's question :

Why is the life of man here in yerthe more wreched sorowful & worse than the lyfe of any other brute beste.

Gyn. Thou knowest . . . that the body of man is more feble and tender than the body of any other brute beste for the bodye of man is all tender and naked . . . for ye fysshes have of theyr nature shelles or skalys to couer and defend theyr bodyes / the bestes be full of here and haue thycke skynnes / the foules haue fethers. . . . Man must take great labour for the obteynynge of his necessary fode & lyuyng as to tyll the grounde . . . to get hym drynk & fode (II. 5). And also the (soul) of man hath a more noble and a more worthy beyng than the brute best whiche hath but lyfe sensytyue (I. 6).

The same fundamental thoughts occur in the *Four Elements* :

> Plantis and herbys growe and be insensate
> Brute bestis have memory and their wyttes fyue
> But thou hast all those and soule intellectyue
> So by reason of thyne understandynge
> Thou hast domynyon of other bestes all.
>
> *Four Elements*, A. 6.

" He that studieth for the life bestial, as voluptuous pleasure and bodily rest, I account him never better than a beast." " The more that thou desirest to know anything, therein thou seemest the more a man to be ; for that man desireth no manner cunning, all that while no better than a beast is he." These two sentences from the speech of Natura Naturata in the *Four Elements*, occur as follows in the words of the Ploughman :

> One cause thereof ys for lak of lernyng
> They perseyue not the reason of the thyng.
> A nother is be cause ther be many
> That call them self gentylmen unworthy
> Whych lyfe voluptuously & bestyall.
>
> *G. and N.*, Book I.

When the Ploughman says that " each man is born to labour truly as a bird is born to fly naturally " he is uttering one of Rastell's principles, one that got him into trouble in later years when he fought the clergy about tithes and offerings.   It is behind the strong views on the evils of inheritance that he maintains in *Gentleness and Nobility*. It is expressed just as clearly in the *Four Elements* :

> For euery man in reason thus ought to do
> To labour for his owne necessary lyuynge
> And than for the welth of his neyghbour also.
>
> *Four Elements*, A. 3.

I have, however, said enough to show my reasons for believing that the play of *Gentleness and Nobility* is the work of John Rastell.   A more exhaustive collection of parallel passages might be made, but it is sufficient to have found typical examples from the *Pastyme of People*, the *Boke of Purgatory*, and the *Four Elements*.

If, then, in the words " Johẽs rastell me fieri fecit " in the colophon of *G. and N.*, we are to understand that authorship is implied, what is the meaning of the colophon of *Calisto and Meleboea*, " Johẽs rastell me imprimi fecit " ?

It would be an important help to know how Rastell himself might render the words, and I think that we have this information.   The colophon to his edition of Lynacre's *Progymnasmata* runs :

Empryntyd in London on yᵉ Sowth syde of Paulys by John Rastell with yᵉ priuylege of our most suverayn lord kyng henry the VIII graunted to the compyler thereof that no man in thys hys realm sell none but such as *the same compyler makyth prynted* for yᵉ space of II yeare.

The italics are mine ;   the words " Johẽs rastell me imprimi fecit " may therefore be rendered on Rastell's authority, " John Rastell (the compyler) had me put in print ".   And they bear the same meaning in his *Magnum Abbreviamentum* of 1528.

The Interlude of *Calisto and Meleboea*, following in the

train of Medwall's *Lucres*, is a comedy of romantic intrigue, and like Medwall's play it is a translation. In Mr. H. Warner Allen's edition of Mabbe's translation of *Celestina* with the Interlude of *Calisto and Meleboea*, we are fortunate in possessing a remarkably comprehensive and methodical treatment of the literary history of this early Spanish picaresque romance. The Interlude, he suggests, was translated directly from the Spanish not earlier than 1502. The translator worked fairly literally on Act I, part of Act II and Act IV of the twenty-one acts of the original. Then after line 920 the connection with the original suddenly ceases, the coarse intrigues of " Celestina the bawd " are cut short, the father of Meleboea enters under a name new to the romance, " Danio ", and the play proceeds to an edifying, moral conclusion. Of the 1,088 lines of the Interlude, 800 were found by Mr. Allen to be more or less literally translated, 168 belong to the moral ending, and there are 42 lines of introductory dialogue before the translation begins. We are left therefore with only 78 lines of original matter in the body of the play. Some of these are scriptural and conventional substitutions for classical references. Eve, for instance, takes the place of an erring goddess; a prayer to St. Appoline is substituted for a Cumaean charm; Meleboea " goeth to mass " prettily in the Interlude, but merely " goes abroad " in the original. There is not much scope left, therefore, for a search for Rastell's workmanship in the body of the translation.

I hope to show, however, that it is not improbable that his hand is to be detected there.

To More, Celestina was " the baude mother of naughtynes ", and the writer of the edifying close was of the same opinion. How was the needful break effected ? A few lines of soliloquy are allowed to Celestina, who then departs to inform Calisto, the Romeo of the " Tragicomedia ", that the plot goes well ; and then Danio, father of Meleboea, enters, greatly haunted by a horrid dream. Meleboea comes on and he relates the dream. She recognizes its significance

I

and confesses how near to disaster she has come. At her
father's bidding she prays for forgiveness ; he raises her up,
and then turning to the audience takes upon him the Rastellian office of philosopher, and begins :

> Lo here ye may see what a thyng it is
> To bryng up yong people verteously,

and we fall back at once into a characteristic vein :

> The bryngers up of youth in this region
> Haue done gret harme because of theyr neclygens
> Not puttyng them to lernyng nor occupacyons
> So when they haue no craft nor sciens
> And come to mans state ye see thexperience
> That many of them compelled be
> To beg or stele by very necessite.

The same complaint of the evil effects of an idle youth
appears in the words of our old friend the Ploughman :

> Alas I haue knowen many or thys
> So proud of theyr byrth that all theyr lyffys
> wold gyf them to no labour nor lernyng
> whych brought them to myserable endyng
> That in pouerte wrechydly dyd dye
> Or fallyn to theft & hangyed therfore full hye.
>
> G. and N., Book I.

And having shown the evil results of the neglect of
education and training, the Rastellian Danio calls on the
" heads and rulers " to make good laws, execute them
straitly and remove the cause of social ills by seeing to it
that young folk are well brought up. Then he concludes :

> Wherfore the eternall god that raynyth on hye
> Send his mercefull grace & influens
> To all gouernours that they circumspectly
> May rule theyr inferiours by such prudence
> To bryng them to vertew & dew Obedyens
> And that they & we all by his grete mercy
> May be parteners of hys blessyd glory.
>   AMEN

> Johēs rastell me imprimi fecit.

The resemblance of the moralizing addresses at the conclusion of *Gentleness and Nobility* and *Calisto and Meleboea*
with their exhortations to " gouernors ", are too striking to
be lightly set aside. We are listening to John Rastell
" singing again his old song ", the song of which we are told
in 1536 that Cranmer was " aweary ".

But if Rastell created the " Danio " close, he must have
invented the dream ; and here again the *Boke of Purgatory*
helps us. Rastell had views on dreams and visions which
he sets forth at length in the sixth chapter of Book II. It
is a long chapter, and we learn from it some unexpected
things, such as that dogs and hogs do not dream in spite
of their noises ; but for our present purpose I will select
a short passage :

Many a man in his dreme hath had dyuers vysyons / and
hath forseen & had knowledge of thynges to come / whych hath
afterwarde fallen playnly and truely accordyng to his vysyon.

Assuming therefore that we have good reason for attributing the unexpected dénouement and moral ending of
the comedy to Rastell, is there any of his handiwork in the
body of the play—that is, in the translation ? There is one
passage at least that is striking ; Calisto is complaining of
the consuming fire of his love, when the translation ceases
and we find the following passage intruded :

> C. And yf the fyre of purgatory bren in such wyse
> I had leuer my spirite in brute bestes shuld be
> Than to go thydyr and than to the deyte
> S. Mary Sir that is a spyce of heryse
> C. why so / S. For ye speke lyke no crystynman.

A similar reference to heresy occurs in *G. and N.* :

Kt. Beware what ye sey sir now I aduyse you for it is treason
or herysy that ye spek now.

But it is the possible reference to the Purgatory controversy
and the Rastellian allusion to brute beasts that arrests us,
for Rastell has much to say in the *Boke of Purgatory* on the

souls of brute beasts. He holds that they are not immortal.
We are not, in that case, dealing with a Pythagorean allusion,
but with an indication of Rastell's influence.

Another case, which is equally striking, occurs in the
translation itself. The Spanish (1502) reads :

No has leydo el filosofo do dize Assi como la materia apetece
als forma assi la muger al varo ?

which Mabbe renders, " Did you never read of that philosopher, where he tells you that, as the matter desires the
form, so woman desires man ? [1]
But we have already seen that Rastell's view of nobility
or worthiness was that it implied absence of dependence,
need or desire (p. 110). So that he changes the obvious
translation to square with his own theory, and instead of
woman desiring man, he renders it woman is less worthy or
noble than man.

Phylozophers say the matter is less worthy
Than the forme / so is woman to man surely.
Cal., A. 4.

Rastell doubtless had friends in the circle of More and
Vives, as well as in Queen Katherine's household, who might
do the translation, but the passage suggests that he revised
it in his capacity as adapter.

The conclusion of my argument, therefore, is that John
Rastell was certainly the author of the *Four Elements*
and *Gentleness and Nobility*, and I believe that he was the
adapter or compiler of *Calisto and Meleboea*. Mr. Allen's
argument that the comedy was translated from the Spanish
is well supported, but no one has yet, apparently, compared
it with the French version of 1527. We have no evidence
as to Rastell's knowledge of Spanish, but his French was
good enough for anything. Baskervill's stimulating and

---

[1] The proposition is common in scholastic philosophy. Chaucer has
" As matier apetiteth form alwey ", L. G. W., 1582. And Hoby's *Courtyer*
has : " It is the opinion of most wise men that man is likened to the Form,
the woman to the Mattier ".

suggestive little article on Rastell's dramatic activities (*Mod. Phil.*, xiii, 1916) [1] comes near to stating my results. Rastell's stage in Finsbury Fields is a fact to be reckoned with.

It is, I repeat, becoming apparent that the break with the tradition of the allegorical morality and the rise of the freer forms of imaginative drama are connected in a remarkable way with the circle of the Rastells, More and Heywood, and it seems that the movement towards dramatic freedom began in the household in which More was brought up, the household of Cardinal Morton.

The problems of the Canon of John Heywood's plays, and their place in the development we have been dealing with, is the subject of my next chapter.

[1] The Rastell authorship of *G. and N.* is ably maintained by Miss E. C. Dunn of Bryn Mawr (*Mod. Lang. Rev.*, 1917), but without reference to the prose works.

CHAPTER V

THE BEGINNINGS OF THE ENGLISH SECULAR AND ROMANTIC DRAMA (II)

THE CANON OF JOHN HEYWOOD'S PLAYS

WHEN John Heywood published his *Woorkes* in 1562, he did not include his plays, and in consequence of this omission there are now doubts as to the authorship of some of the Interludes that a long tradition has attributed to him. *John Heywoodes Woorkes* were, in fact, only the proverbs and epigrams that he had been publishing at intervals since 1546. It is now proposed to determine, if possible, the origin of the traditional canon.

In the first or Ipswich Edition of the *Scriptorum Summarium* of 1548, Bale mentions only the first two books of the Proverbs, *atque alia*.

In the second or Basle Edition of 1557 he mentions three plays, *De Aura* (*Wether*), *De Amore* (*Love*) and *De Quadruplici P.* (*The Four PP.*)

Pitseus, in his *De illustribus Angliae Scriptoribus*, published in 1619, added to Bale's list the *Spider and the Flie* and a book of English songs, " et alia his similia non pauca ", but he did not add any new plays.

In 1671 Francis Kirkman revised a list of plays appended in 1661 to his edition of *Tom Tyler*, and printed it at the end of his edition of John Dancer's translation of Corneille's *Nicomède*, as " an exact catalogue of all the English Stage Plays printed till this present year 1671 . . . all of which you may either buy or sell at the house of Francis Kirkman in Thames Street, over against the Custom House, London ". This list is arranged alphabetically under titles, the *Four*

PP. coming under F and the rest of the Heywood plays under P, as follows :

p. 5. John Heywood, Four PP. I (Interlude).
p. 11. John Heywood, Play of Love. I.
   John Heywood, Play of Weather. I.
   John Heywood, Play between Johan Johan the husband, Tib his wife etc. I.
   John Heywood, Play between the Pardoner and the Friar, the Curate and Neighbour Prat. I.
   John Heywood, Play of Gentleness and Nobility, 1st Part. I.
p. 12. John Heywood, Play of Gentleness and Nobility, 2nd Part. I.
   Pinner of Wakefield. C (Comedy)
   Philotas Scotch. C.
H. H. B. Plutus.
   Patient Grissil.
   Patient Grissel old.
   Promises of God manifested.
   Promos and Cassandra, 1st Part.

I have given the list in its original form (1671 edition) because it explains a curious blunder made by Phillips, Winstanley, and Anthony à Wood, and, strangely, copied by Warton a century later. These all add to Kirkman's list of Heywood's plays the impossible *Pinner of Wakefield* (*George-a-Green*) and a Scottish *Philotas*. It will be seen from the paging and arrangement given above to be a natural blunder to treat the anonymous plays as covered by the last writer mentioned.

There are three earlier Play Lists each printed like this as an appendix to a quarto edition of a play. They are found in

A. Rogers and Ley's edition of *The Careless Shepherdess*, 1656.
B. Archer's edition of *The Old Law*, 1656.
C. Kirkman's First List in his edition of *Tom Tyler*, 1661.

So far as Heywood is concerned, Kirkman's first list does not differ from his second of ten years later ; Rogers and Ley

Then follow the *Four PP.*, possibly his own copy, for he quotes Middleton's title-page, *Johan Johan, Pardoner and Frere, Gentleness and Nobility* (two parts), *Love*, and *Wether*. He adds : " Dr. Fuller mentions a Book writ by our author entitled ' Monumenta Literaria ' which is said to be ' non tam labore condita quam lepore condita ' ".[1]

He then corrects the blunder of Phillips and Winstanley.

'Tis not unlikely that our Author may have more Plays in Print than we have mentioned ; but I am very confident that the Pinder of Wakefield and Philotos Scotch, notwithstanding the Allegations of Mr Phillips and Mr Winstanley are not of that number ; the one being written, as I suppose, at least printed above 20, the other more than 40 years after his death.[2]

ANTHONY À WOOD, *Athenae Oxoniensis* (1691), follows Phillips and Winstanley, including in his list the *Pinner* and *Philotas*. He adds that he had also seen an *Interlude of Youth* printed in London in old English characters, *temp*. Henry. VIII, but whether John Heywood was the author of it he does not know.

Wood adds several well-known biographical notes from Bale, Pits, Peacham, Harington, and Camden.

THOMAS WARTON, *Hist. Eng. Poet.* (vol. iii, 1781), follows Wood, and therefore, not to his credit, retains the *Pinner* and *Philotas*, apparently disregarding Langbaine.

DAVID ERSKINE BAKER,[3] *Biographia Dramatica* (1782), gives the six plays and adds bibliographical descriptions.

He rejects *Pinner* and *Philotas*, saying :

Langbaine rejects their authority (Phillips and Winstanley) and I think with good authority, as both these pieces are printed anonymous and both of them not published until upwards of 30 years after the author's death.

---

[1] Fuller's reference to *Monumenta Literaria* is due to a quaint and rather stupid mishandling of Pitseus, " De Joanne Heyvode " : " non pauca tradidit posteris literaria monumenta non tam labore condita quam lepore condita " (p. 753).

[2] A note in Langbaine explains the Scottish *Philotas* : " Philotas, a Comedy 4to printed in Scotland, 1612. The Play shows the mischief oftimes happening by old age marrying with Youth." By a curious coincidence this is the theme of Part II of Heywood's *Dialogue*. Rogers and Ley (1656) call it *Philotas in Scotch*.

[3] Defoe's grandson.

It is not necessary to carry the early history of the canon farther. So far as the plays are concerned, the traditional canon assumed its present form in the book-shop of Francis Kirkman. Phillips used Kirkman's list and blundered into adding the *Pinner* and *Philotas*. Langbaine corrected the blunder and Baker accepted the correction, but Winstanley, Wood and Warton followed Phillips.

Thus, whatever we may think of the judgment of critics who could include *George-a-Greene, the Pinner of Wakefield*, in Heywood's works, it is important that we should recognize that Kirkman was innocent. What grounds he had for definitely assigning *Johan Johan* and the *Pardoner and Frere* to Heywood we cannot say, but, in spite of his loose terms, " the first English Play-writer ", " the first English printing ", he bought and sold and lent and loved his plays and romances, and the judgment of the generation that produced a Junius and a Dryden is not to be despised, though it may leave us problems.

There are thus six plays assigned by tradition to Heywood, and we are able to add to that number the manuscript play at the British Museum commonly known as *Witty and Witless*, which is subscribed " qth Jhon Heywood ", but which was unknown to the bookseller, Kirkman.

The play of *Love* and the play of *Wether* were printed by Heywood's brother-in-law, Wm. Rastell, who states on the title-page that they are by John Heywood. The manuscript play may also with certainty be accepted as Heywood's.[1]

The *Pardoner and Frere* and *Johan Johan* were also printed by Wm. Rastell, but they have no title-page, the title occurring as a descriptive heading on the first page of the play ; moreover, they are anonymous. The *Four PP.*

---

[1] The manuscript play *Witty and Witless* (Harl. 367) in laborious closeness of debate resembles *Love*, and has many affinities of style with that play and *Wether*. Though the MS. concludes, " Amen qth John Heywood ", it is not in Heywood's hand. (See facsimiles, p. 124.) For the dates of Rastell's editions of the Heywood plays see p. 81.

was printed by Wm. Middleton, a printer of law and medical books, about 1544, with a title-page on which the play is said to have been " made by John Heywood ".[1]

It appears, therefore, that of Kirkman's six plays the position in the Canon of two is secure beyond all question. *Love* and *Wether* are stated in 1533 to be Heywood's by his brother-in-law, Wm. Rastell, and are recorded by Bale in 1557, Pitseus in 1619, and Kirkman in 1661.[2]

The *Four PP.* has a very good claim to inclusion, one indeed that can only be set aside if it is found to be unreasonable to suppose that Heywood wrote the play. Middleton (*c.* 1544), Bale (1557), Pitseus (1619), and Kirkman (1661) all show Heywood as the author.

Johan Johan and the *Pardoner and the Frere* have no particular affinities of style or matter with *Love* and *Wether*, but obvious affinities with the *Four PP.* and with one another. If it should prove that the *Four PP.* is not a Heywood play, it would be very difficult to retain *Johan Johan* and the *Pardoner and the Frere*, as they do not come into the traditional Canon until 1661. *Gentleness and Nobility* we have claimed for John Rastell.

We are, therefore, confronted with a pretty problem. There are two trilogies claimed for Heywood which are remarkably unlike, so unlike at a first glance that they appear to be the work of different minds.

The *Love* group is undoubtedly Heywood's, and its characteristics are found also in the *Dialogue*, the *Spider and the Flie*, and the Ballads and Songs.

The subject-matter of the other group stands apart from Heywood's unquestioned work. We find, for instance, among the undoubted works nothing in the spirit of the *Pardoner and the Frere*, nothing resembling, let us say, More's *Mery jest of how a Sergeant would play the Frere*, which is quite in that spirit. There is, indeed, one

---

[1] Of the thirty-seven dated works printed by Middleton only three appeared before 1543. The *Four PP.* is his only known play.

[2] See p. 119.

HEYWOOD'S HAND AND THE MS. OF 'WITTY AND WITLESS'
(a) FROM THE MS. OF THE PLAY (see p. 123 n.)
(b) HEYWOOD'S HAND IN 1575 (see p. 37)
(c) HIS SIGNATURE TO A LEASE IN 1539 (see p. 57)

passage in the *Spider and the Flie* that has the older satiric note :

> There never was Fryer limiter, that duckt,
> So low, where beggyng woon him twenty cheeses,
> As is the flie now to the spider ruckte.

But Kirkman characterized Heywood's plays as " making notable work with the then clergy ". " The then clergy " do not appear in *Love* or *Wether*, nor does *Witty and Witless* contain any reference to them. He must, in fact, have referred to the *Four PP.* group. Are we, then, safe in accepting Middleton's title-page and attributing the *Four PP.* to John Heywood ?

Middleton, the printer of the *Four PP.*, began to print about 1541, and died in 1547, during which time he printed many law books and some medical works. He was buried at St. Dunstan's in the West (P.C. Wills, 39 Alen). His shop was at the Sign of the George in Fleet Street, and his customers were probably mostly from the Inns of Court and Chancery near at hand. Richard and John Heywood's houses in St. Bride's Parish and Salisbury Court were almost within a stone's throw of his shop, and the *Four PP.* first saw the light in a part of London where few men were better known than the Heywoods and their friends, the Ropers, Rastells, and their legal circle.

In 1543 the Commission of Enquiry into the plot against Cranmer began its investigations, and, as we have already shown, John Heywood very narrowly escaped the death of a traitor at Tyburn by submitting to read a recantation at Paul's Cross in July 1544. I think it is reasonable to assume that Middleton printed the *Four PP.* while Heywood's case was the talk of the Inns of Court. When a book or pamphlet is issued in such circumstances one usually sees plainly the action either of a friend or of a foe. I submit that Middleton's enterprise was not merely an attempt to catch a ready market, but was calculated to do Heywood good. It certainly was no hostile act. For what was the charge against him ? His recantation shows that his complicity in the reactionary plot of Gardiner, Norfolk and the enemies of Cranmer was reduced to a charge of denial of the King's Supremacy. The play, of course, does not touch the question of the Supremacy, but it shows Heywood as the satirist of the parasites of the old order, and if I am right in my view of the circumstances and time of the publication, it is clear that the act of printing was not an unfriendly one.

Without going so far as to assert that Heywood was responsible for the act of publication, one may suggest that his friends undertook or prompted it. In that case the credentials of the title-page would be as good as those of *Love* and *Wether*.

But assuming as an alternative that the enterprise was entirely due to Middleton's quick business instinct, then we are met by certain possibilities. Either he knew the play to be a Heywood play, or he was ignorant in the matter, or he knew it was not a Heywood play.

In the first case, the title-page would be a statement of fact ; in the second and third cases we must charge Middleton with an act of clever dishonesty.

But what need was there for dishonesty ? The *Four PP.* is a good piece of work. It was reprinted by Copland and Allde, and it had no need of the added attraction of Heywood's name. Further we have, so far as I know, no reason to look upon Middleton as a dishonest man. The list of his works in Mr. A. W. Pollard's Hand List does not support the suggestion of dishonesty. There is therefore apparently no particular reason for supposing Middleton's title-page to be suspect. If, however, we can show from an examination of the play that it contains clear evidence of Heywood's mannerisms and methods, then I think that we may consider that the title-page is reliable and the play Heywood's.

The *Four PP.*, like *Love, Witty and Witless* and *Wether*, is a " debate ". The question at issue is not, as Collier suggests, which can tell the greatest lie, but whether the

Palmer, the Pardoner or the Potycary " shall take the best place ".

The office of each is to send folk to heaven, or as the Arbiter, the Pedlar, puts it :

> Eche of you somwhat doth showe
> That soules towards heven by you do growe.

Why not, he suggests, " agree to contynue togyther all thre, and all obey one wyll ? " The Palmer might discharge men of their pilgrimages, the Pardoner grant folk indulgences, and the Potycary send them to heaven. But such co-operation demands a leadership :

> " For good order," says that Potycary,
> " Twayne of us must wayte on the thryde."

This question of precedence being raised, the arbiter devises as tests of supremacy :

> some maner thynge
> Wherin ye all be lyke connynge,

" even lying ", for :

> all ye can lye as well
> as can the falsest devyll in hell.

Here the position is like that of the *Spider and the Flie*, who, having stated their cases before the two arbiters, Antony Ant and Bartilmew Butterfly, it is found that the decision depends on the relative " credence " or honesty of spiders and flies—in a word, which is to be believed, a point in legal practice that troubled Solomon (see *Spider and Flie*, cap. 38 ff.). On this question of the relative honesty the case breaks down before the arbiters, and civil war ensues.

In the *Four PP.*, with comic irony, the claims to precedence of the three disputants are decided not by the test of credibility, but of incredibility or mendacity.

I would therefore suggest that the central theme is in Heywood's manner.

So also is the conclusion characteristic of Heywood, for though the Palmer's lie is adjudged " to be the most excellent ", the other two refuse to acknowledge his lordship, and in the language as it might be of the Chamberlain of the Household, the victor discharges his truculent subordinates :

> I clearly of waiting do discharge ye.

For one characteristic of a Heywood debate is that it never reaches a decision, unless by the interposition of a *deus ex machina*. Thus Jerome shifts the ground and closes the discussion between John and James in *Witty and Witless* ; Jupiter's fiat closes the debate of *Wether* ; *Love* ends in a compromise and a Christmas wish ; the *Spider and the Flie* is closed by the Maid (Mary) who, with a sweep of her broom, clears the lattice of cobwebs and ends a controversy of ninety-eight chapters.

And in this same manner the Pedlar decides :

> Now be ye all evyn as ye begoon
> No man hath loste nor no man hath woon.

On the contrary, it is a strong argument against Kirkman's attribution of *Gentleness and Nobility* to Heywood that the writer leaves us in no doubt as to his decision, viz. that it is " virtue and gentle conditions " alone that make " gentleness and nobility ". He even lectures the worshipful audience, " Souereyns all that here present be ", warning them that their

> hedys rulers and gouernours all
> Shuld come therto because of theye vertue,
> And in auctoryte they ought not contynue
> Except they be good men, dyscrete and wyse
> And haue a loue and zele unto Justyce.

In Heywood's *débats* there occurs a characteristic summing-up or recapitulation of the case already stated at length by the parties to the controversy. These recapitulations are somewhat frequent in a long work like the *Spider and the Flie*, and they add to its tediousness.   Cap. 23 may be cited as a typical case.   In *Wether*, Merry Report recapitulates the claims of the eight suitors carefully and at length (D iii verso and iv recto) ; James, in *Witty and Witless*, summarizes the earlier arguments for Jerome (p. 205, Farmer's *E.E. Drama*).

It appears to have been beyond even Heywood's powers to present a summary of the arguments used in *Love*, and although the slow movement of the play is due in part to repeated retrogressions, no single recapitulation is possible.

In the *Four PP.* the Pardoner's recapitulation of the claims and arguments of the Palmer, the Pardoner, and the Potycary is quite carefully done and is not at all unlike the rehearsal in Cap. 23 of the *Spider and the Flie*.   It occurs at the close of the part song and serves to start the debate again.

At first sight it might be imagined that a comparison of the place-names in the *Four PP.* with those in *Wether* would be of assistance in determining the question of authorship.   Merry Report's list in *Wether* is, however, merely a list alliterating in threes :

> At Taunton at Tiptree at Tottenham.

Essex names predominate, and it ends with the reference to the Heywood village.   Otherwise the places are selected for alliteration only.   In all its forty places it has only two shrines, Walsingham and Canterbury.   In fact, Merry Report, the Vice, though he " seek strange strondes ", is not a Palmer so much as a Puck.

The Palmer, on the other hand, tells of his pilgrimages to Rome, to Rhodes, to St. Mark's, to the Armenian Hills where he saw the Ark, to the great shrines of England and Wales and even to St. Patrick's Purgatory, but the author works for an amusing climax, and in this the methods of the two plays are alike.

Merry Report ends his list of travels with

> Ynge Gyngiang Jayberd, Parish of Butsbery ;

K

The Palmer's record closes :

> At Crome at Wyldsdone and at Muswell
> At Saynt Rycharde and at Saynt Roke
> And at our lady that standeth in the oke.[1]

The two lists, in fact, though unlike in kind, show the same feeling for climax and follow the same method in attaining it.

The *Four PP.* opens with seven quatrains rhyming alternately, and closes with two stanzas in rhyme royal ; the rest of the play is in couplets. Love opens and closes in rhyme royal, but most of the play is in couplets.

The interludes have in common a trick of continuing the rhyme of a couplet over a quatrain or more of lines, sometimes in a rhyming bout, but often in soliloquy. Thus :

> *Potycary.* Than tell me thys be ye perfyt in drynkynge
> *Pedler.* Perfyt in drynkynge as may be wyshte by thynkyng
> *Potycary.* Then after your drynkyng how fall ye to wynkyng
> *Pedler.* Syr after drynkynge whyle the shot is tynkynge
> Some hedes be swymmyng but myne wyl be synkynge
> And upon drynkynge myne eyse wyll be pynkynge
> For wynkyng to drynkynge is alway lynkynge.
> *(Four PP.*, B ii recto.)

[1] The necessity for a rhyme accounts for the intrusion of St. Roc Amadour among these London shrines. Crome was on Crome Hill, near the Royal palace of Greenwich ; St. Richard's was at St. Paul's ; Muswell, Willesden, and our Lady of the Oak (Highgate Woods) were shrines in the Middlesex Forest whose booths and stalls were familiar to all Londoners. These local shrines had a doubtful reputation. In 1531 one John Harris, draper, said they were as bad as " Stew-side," and had to abjure his charge. In 1538, however, Cromwell had all the " notable images " destroyed at Chelsea " unto which were made any special pilgrimages and offerings . . . as the ladie of Willesden " (see *Lond. and Middlesex Arch. Trans.*, iv, 173, and Prickett's *Highgate*). The list of shrines in the Palmer's speech deserves further attention, but as it does not bear upon my general argument I will only mention that the shrine of Master John Shorne, who conjured the devil into a boot, was transferred to Windsor in 1478, where also the shrine of King Harry stood (see *Norf. Arch.*, ii, 280). I might add that offerings at three of the other shrines are mentioned in the Earl of Devon's accounts in 1518, viz. the Rood of St. Uncumber, Our Lady of Crome, and St. George of Southwark (R.O., Misc. Bks., T.R., 219).

Palmer.   Then wolde some mayster perhappes clowte ye
But as for me ye nede nat doute ye
For I had lever be without ye
Then have suche besynesse about ye.
                              (*Four PP.*, C ii verso.)

There are twelve other well-marked cases in the play.
In *Love* there are eight instances, but for comparison I
select two :

No (*ther*) *lover nor loved.*   Nowe god you good evyn mayster
        woodcock.
Lover loved.   Cometh of rudeness or lewednesse that mock.
No lover nor loved.   Come whereof it shall ye come of such stock,
        That god you good evyn mayster woodcock.
                              (*Love*, B i recto.)

No lover nor loved.   My harte mysgave me by god that bought me
        That if she myst me where I thought she sought me
        She sewer wolde be madde by love that she ought me
        Wherin not love, but pity so wrought me
        That to retourne anone I bethought me
        And so returned tyll chaunce had brought me
        To her chambre dore.
                              (*Love*, C i recto.)

There are similar cases in *Witty and Witless,* but none in
Gentleness and Nobility if we except one instance in Part I
and four in Part II of dissyllables rhyming on the suffix,
e.g. " rulers, teachers, officers, executors ", which is not
the same thing.   It should be mentioned that, with the
exception of the Epilogue, *Gentleness and Nobility* is in
couplets.

A curious mark of Heywood's exuberance appears in
Love ; it is less marked in *Witty and Witless,* it occurs in
a modified form in the songs and is not found in *Wether.*
It takes the form of a playful reiteration of a word which
he worries and tosses as a puppy worries a rag.

Thus in *Love* :

    Thus tyme out of tyme mystymeth my rate
    For tyme to bring tyme to hope of any grace
    That tyme tymeth no tyme in any tyme or place.
                              (A ii verso.)

M.R.   How spend ye the nyght
G.   In daunsynge and syngynge
     Tyll mydnyght and then fall to slepynge
M.R.   Why swete herte by your false fayth can ye syng
G.   Nay nay but I love yt above all thynge

(I here omit five lines.)

M.R.   Come on syrs but now let us synge lustily

(Here they synge.)

G.   Syr this is well done I hertely thanke you
     Ye have done me pleasure I make god avowe
     Ones in a nyght I long for suche a fyt
     For longe tyme have I ben brought up in it.
           (*Wether*, C iv verso and D recto.)

In the *Four PP.* the talk leads from drinking and sleeping to singing, in *Wether* from dancing and sleeping to singing. In both cases there follows the question, " Can you sing ? " Then comes the lead, " Come on syrs, let us synge lustily ", or " who that lyste synge after me " ; finally the approval, " This is well done ", " This liketh me well ".[1]

As bearing on this question of single authorship, I would draw attention to the stage fooling of the Potycary in the *Four PP.* and the Vice in *Love* :

Potycary.   By the masse lerne to make curtesy
     Curtesy before and curtesy behynde hym
     And then on eche syde.
           (E ii verso.)

No lover nor loved.   And nowe I am here before you
     And nowe I am here behynd ye
     And nowe we be here evyn both together
     And now be we welcome evyn both hyther
     Syns nowe ye fynde me here with curtsy I may
     Byd you welcome hyther as I may say.
           (C ii recto.)

---

[1] The song in *Fulgens and Lucres* is an essential part of the competition of A and B for the hand of the Maid. Medwall makes dramatic use of his song. Rastell introduces into the *Four Elements* a troupe of dancers to sing the song he prints.

Two other points may be added :

(a) References to St Anthony :

No lover nor loved. They shall have a beck by seynt Antony
But alas good maysters I crye you mercy.
                    (*Love,* C iii verso.)

Mery report. My lorde how now loke uppe lustely
Here is a derlinge come by saynt Antony.
                    (*Wether,* C iii recto.)

Potycary. Yes that I wyll by saynt Antony
And by the leve of thys company
Prove ye false knaves.
                    (*Four PP.,* A iii verso.)

Pardoner.   but by saynt Antony
I wene he hath sent you to muche all redy.
                    (*Four PP.,* C ii verso.)

Pardoner.   and by saynt Antony
He smyled on me well favored.
                    (*Four PP.,* D iii verso.)

(b) " glyster " :

For at all tymys when suche thynges shall myster
my new hed shall geve myne olde tayle a glyster.
                    (*Wether,* B ii recto.)

That way perchaunce ye shall nat myster
To go to heven without a glyster.
                    (*Four PP.,* A iv recto.)

Yet dyd I take more payne about her
Then I wolde take with my owne syster
Syr at the last I gave her a glyster.
                    (*Four PP.,* D i recto.)

If I may assume that these illustrations of Heywood's
tricks of style are sufficient to justify us in accepting Middleton's ascription of the play to him, one is inclined to think
of him as the author of the two anonymous plays, the
Pardoner and Frere and *Johan Johan*, although one misses
in *Johan Johan* Heywood's mannerisms. Such tests, for
instance, as I have applied in the case of the *Four PP.*
have failed me in the case of *Johan Johan.*

On the other hand, this play conforms to the type of the group ; it " makes notable work with the then clergy ", and therein it departs from the French farce with which it has been connected. (K. Young, *Mod. Phil.*, 1904, ii).

In *Pernet qui va au vin* the lover is simply a " Cousin, un Amoureux ". A further departure from the French brings it still closer into harmony with its group ; *Johan Johan* ends in a scuffle like the *Pardoner and Frere* (and More's *Mery Jest*), whereas *Pernet* ends weakly in submission.

> *Pernet.* C'est ung tres povre passetemps
> De chauffer (la) cire quant on digne.
> Regardez ; elle est plus molle que laine.
> En la chauffant rien n'aqu-este.
>
> *Le Cousin.* Conclus et conqueste ;
> Avec la femme je banqueste.
> Combien que je ne sois le sire
> Et son mary chauffe la cire.
>   (Finis.)

The isolation of the trilogy in the early Tudor drama is a remarkable fact. No other interludes handle its themes, and, indeed, one might extend the field and say that there is nothing of kindred subject in early Tudor verse.

One outstanding exception, however, is to be noted. More's *Mery Jest*, which, according to William Rastell, was written in his youth, is quite in the spirit of the *Pardoner and Frere*.

There are, of course, rude tales of wanton friars and their kind in the 100 *Mery Tales* printed by John Rastell, and the similar " jest books " that W. C. Hazlitt collected and reprinted. The poem of More's youth stands, however, with the trilogy in isolation ; left, as it were, by the receding tide of mediaevalism, but caught and refloated in the counterflow of the Renaissance. And just as William Rastell saved the *Mery Jest*, so too it was he who printed the *Pardoner and Frere* and *Johan Johan*.

The metre of More's verses is the well-known metre of the *Nut Brown Maid*, a stanza said by Schipper, however, to be uncommon in Middle English. He only cites a poem of Dunbar's, and alludes to continental models in Low Latin, Provençal, and Old French (*Hist. Eng. Vers.*, par. 244).

More's *Mery Jest* is of a " sergeant-at-law who would learn to playe the frere ". To outwit a merchant he assumes a disguise :

and for a day
all his array
} he changed with a frere

But the merchant turned the tables on his visitor :

and with his fist
upon the lyst
} he gave hym such a blow
That backward downe
Almost in sowne
} the frere is overthrow

The Wife and Maid then enter to complete the discomfiture. They pull the friar's hood down about his face and

while he was blynde
The wench behynde
} lent hym, leyd on the flore,
Many a soule
about the noule
} with a great batyldore

The conclusion points to the poem having been written as a prologue or welcome to a feast or entertainment to be used in the manner of an interlude :

Now masters all
Here now I shall
} Ende there as I began
In any wise
I would avyse
} and counsayle every man
His own craft use
All newe refuse
} and lyghtly let them gone
Play not the frere
Now make good cheere
} and welcome everych one

The question arises whether More's influence may not be seen in the *Pardoner and Frere* ; for besides their affinity of theme, the play and the poem have this interesting

feature in common, that on two occasions the dialogue
of the play drops into the metre of More's poems :

Frere. But first of all
Now here I shall   } to God my prayer make
To give ye grace
All in this place   } His doctrine for to take.

Here the Frere falls on his knees, and the Pardoner entering,
addresses the audience and concludes :

And because ye
Shall unto me   } give credence at the full
Mine auctoritee
Now shall ye see   } Lo ! here the Pope's bull.

Heywood's use of the same stanza in a ballad printed
as a broadsheet by Allde (N.D.), and entitled *A Ballad
against Detraction,* strikes one as being quite different in
manner :

Lyke as a knyfe
Berevyth life   } so sklandre some hath slayne
And both once doone
Both alike soone   } may be undoone agayne.

I have perhaps said enough to show that More's influence
on Heywood is more demonstrable than it might appear
to be. The trilogy as a group is characterized by its spirit
of anti-clerical banter. One of its plays, the *Four PP.,*
almost certainly contains Heywood's work, and it is generally
accepted that it is closely related to the *Pardoner and Frere*
(see Hillebrand, *Mod. Phil.,* Sept. 1915). This latter play,
however, and indeed the whole group, are more closely related
to what is known to be More's work than to Heywood's
other work. I would suggest, therefore, that, although the
common spirit of the three plays may point to single authorship, this is due rather to the intimate relationship of Heywood and More ; and that when More introduced his young
protégé to Court in 1519, Heywood's early success was in
no small measure due to this intimacy.

It should be remembered in this connection that Pitseus includes in his list of More's works

Comoediae iuveniles Lib. un.

and Erasmus told von Hutton that as a young man More wrote and took part in *Comoediolas*.

It would be natural to omit the author's name from the *Pardoner and Frere* and *Johan Johan*, if they were More's rather than Heywood's, yet it would also be natural that they should issue from Wm. Rastell's press along with Haywood's two plays.

More resigned the Chancellorship in 1532, and in April 1534 was sent to the Tower. The *Pardoner and Frere* is dated 8th April, 1533, and *Johan Johan* [1] 2nd February, 1533. These dates suggest a comparison with the circumstances of the publication of the *Four PP*.

In the first part of this chapter the history of the Canon was traced, and the plays attributed to John Heywood by a long tradition were found to arrange themselves in two trilogies. It was shown that there was no doubt as to the authorship of *Wether*, *Love*, and *Witty and Witless*, but the evidence supporting the traditional ascription to Heywood of the other trilogy, *Four PP.*, *Pardoner and Frere*, and *Johan Johan*, was found to be less convincing. Much depended on the degree of assurance with which the *Four PP*. might be claimed for the dramatist. This question was discussed in some detail, and it was found that the claim for Heywood rested on good evidence, both external and internal. It was suggested, however, that the *Four PP*. trilogy bore the marks of the influence of the dramatist's older friend and patron, Sir Thomas More. I next propose to consider the problem of the date of the *Four PP*. and the bearing of this on the question of authorship.

It will be remembered by readers of the play that the Potycary refers in the story of his wonderful cure to the loss of the good ship *Regent*.

[1] For the question of dating see p. 81.

Potycary. This tampion flew X longe myle levell
To a fayre castell of lyme and stone
For strength I know not suche a one
Whiche stode upon an hyll full hye
At fote wherof a ryver ranne bye
So depe tyll chaunce had it forbyden
Well myght the regent there have ryden

In August 1512 Wolsey wrote to Fox that there had been a severe sea fight near Brest on Tuesday fortnight, where the *Regent* captured the great carrick of Brest, but, both, fouling, were burnt and most part of the crews with them. Sir Thomas Knyvet and Sir John Carewe had perished. He begs he will keep the news secret. The French fleet had fled to Brest. Sir Edward Howard had vowed " that he will never see the king in the face till he has avenged the death of the noble and valiant knight, Sir Thomas Knyvet " (B.M., Titus B., i, 99).

The *Regent* [1] was probably the biggest ship added by Henry VII to the Navy. She was of 1,000 tons, was built in 1487, and was well known to Londoners (*Navy Records*, vol. 8). A drawing in colours showing the two ships aflame forms the frontispiece of *Navy Records*, vol. 10. Out of her crew of over 700 only 180 escaped, and but six from the carrick, the *Cordelière.*

We are told that Henry seemed unperturbed by the result of the " drowning " of the carrick, and rewarded the messenger with £10. This indication of the King's character is significant. He was twenty-one.

The impression made by the tragic end of the *Regent* may be gathered from contemporary chronicles.

The *Chronicle of the Grey Friars*, under the year 1512–13, records :

This year the king went to France and the carrick and the Regent burnt and this year was the Scottish Field and the king " tane and slayne ".

[1] In Hickscorner, which was probably written before the disaster, the *Regent* heads the list of ships.

But as late as 1520 the loss of the *Regent* was greatly exciting the interest of More and his friends, and in dating the play this has importance.[1]

It has been argued that the " relics " passages in the *Four PP.* are developed from those in the *Pardoner and Frere*,[2] and with this conclusion there is probably considerable agreement. Assuming, then, that this is so, the allusion to Leo X (1513–21) in the latter play calls for attention. It is true that the playful exaggeration of the passage reduces its value. We have, indeed, quite a jumble of Popes : Julius the Sixth has yet to exist, Boniface the Ninth belonged to the fourteenth century, whilst there is an Innocent and a second Julius whom we cannot identify.

It is, however, with the express sanction of Leo X that the Pardoner opens his appeal to his congregation, commissioned by him to grant indulgences to all who shall give alms for the restoration of the chapel of " sweet St. Leonard, that late by fire was destroyed and marred ".[3]

It was in 1517 that Leo X had authorized the famous sale of indulgences to all who would contribute money to the building of St. Peter's. The farcical satire, therefore, of the *Pardoner and Frere* would be received with full popular appreciation if the play appeared when Pope Leo's pardoners were becoming troublesome. The play might be placed, on such assumption, about 1519.

[1] The reference to the loss of the Regent in the *Four PP.* is capable of a pretty explanation if my suggestion of More's interest in the play is sound. The vessel went down in 1512, some eight years before the play is thought to have been written. Can this date (1520) be reconciled with reference to a disaster then no longer of recent occurrence ?   To More and his friends the disaster had not been allowed to pass out of mind.   German de Brie, Secretary to the French Queen, had written a poem eulogizing the French for their part in the disaster, and More had retorted in several epigrams which appeared in a collected edition in 1518.   Annoyed by this, de Brie replied by a critical exposure of alleged lapses in More's *Epigrammata*, and More retorted in an *Epistola ad Germanum Brisium* in 1520.   Both flyters were friends of Erasmus, who interposed in 1520 and stopped the feud.

[2] Hillebrand (*Mod. Phil.*, September 1915).

[3] Some searcher more fortunate than I may perhaps solve the problem of the date of the *Pardoner and Frere* by finding a record of the burning of St. Leonard's Chapel.

The sale of indulgences by Leo X had, however, excited opposition of a much more significant character in Germany. On the eve of All Saints, 1517, Luther nailed his ninety-five theses against indulgences on the door of the palace church at Wittenburg. But Luther's revolt took time to spread, and it was not until 1521 that Henry VIII felt called upon to register a regal protest and publish his *Defence of the Seven Sacraments*.

It is obvious, therefore, that, should a Court dramatist produce a " Pardoner " play while the King was in this very orthodox mood, he would define his position with considerable clearness, and leave his audience in no doubt as to the correctness of his attitude.

Now this is just what we find in the elaborate and lengthy conclusion of the *Four PP*.

The Pedlar sums up the whole matter at issue in a speech beginning :

> Now be ye all evyn as ye begoon
> No man hath loste nor no man hath woon.

First, addressing the Palmer, he declares that he who " for love of Christ " uses to go on pilgrimage spends his time well. The motive is all. To the Pardoner he says that he is working to the same end as the Palmer :

> If ye procure thus indulgence
> Unto your neyghbours charytably
> For love of them is god onely.

And so it is with all who " by ayde of goddes grace " follow any kind of virtue, whether " great almyse for to gyve ", or " in wylfull poverte to lyve ", or to make " hye wayes and suche other workes ", or " to mayntayne prestes and clarkes to synge and praye for souls departed ". Though these virtues be of " sundry kyndes ", yet if men are moved by " love and dred obediently " to work " unyformely in them, they are pleasaunt to God and thankful to man ". But if by " grace of the Holy Goste " a man be moved speci-

ally to one virtue let him beware of " despising other ",
for he perceives that to be the sin of the Palmer and the
Pardoner.

> One kynde of vertue to dyspyse another
> Is like as the syster myght hange the brother.

Here the Potycary rejoices that he has escaped such perils
by " using no vertues at all ", wherefore he is rebuked by
the Pedlar, who, however, sees in the truthfulness of his
remark " one syne of vertue ". Yet he adds significantly,

> I dare well reporte
> Ye are well beloved of all thys sorte
> By your raylynge here openly
> At pardons ond relyques so leudly.

The Potycary retorts :

> In that I thynke my faute not great
> For all that he hath I knowe conterfete.

In a passage quite in Heywood's style, the Pedlar replies
that he is not constrained to reverence what he knows to
be feigned.

> But where ye dout the truthe nat knowynge
> Bilevynge the beste good may be growynge
> In iudgynge the beste no harme at the leste
> In iudgynge the worste no good at the beste
>
> .   .   .   .   .
>
> But as the churche doth iudge or take them
> So do ye receyve or forsake them
> And so be sure ye can nat erre
> But may be a fruitfull follower.

The three disputants acknowledge the excellence of the
Pedlar's counsel and promise amendment, and Heywood
then closes the play in two stanzas of rhyme royal in-
voking all

> To beleve hys churche faste and faythfully
> So that we may accordynge to hys promyse
> Be kepte out of errour in any wyse.

And all that hath scapet us here by neglygence
We clerely revoke and forsake it
To pass the tyme in thys without offence
Was the cause why the maker dyd make it
And so we humbly beseche you to take it
Besechynge our lorde to prosper you all
In the fayth of hys church universall.

I have quoted extensively here because it seems to me worth suggesting that the dramatist is definitely asserting a position in harmony with that of the "Defender of the Faith". I would therefore not feel any necessity to place the *Four PP.* earlier than the date of Henry's book. I think, however, that it was probably not separated very far from the *Pardoner and Frere* and would assign it to 1520–2.

I have already dealt with Dr. Wallace's summary of the life of Heywood. In his treatment of the Heywood Canon he boldly eliminates the *Four PP.*, the *Pardoner and Frere*, and *Johan Johan*, which he equally boldly attributes to the "Octavian Shakespeare", Wm. Cornyshe, the Master of the Chapel children. Cornyshe, he holds, framed the "new style drama" in the "first plastic years of Henry VIII, and that drama was a square break from the past". He repudiates the notion that Heywood was a "link", a "transition", or "a bridge". There is in his view no bridge, but a square break, and Cornyshe is the great originator.

Nothing is known of Cornyshe's writings except his lament entitled *Truth and Information* and some ditties which are quite short. *Truth and Information*, written in prison, deals with his sorrows in the abstract terms familiar in the Moral Interludes. Little as this may imply, it is nevertheless just from those abstractions that he is supposed to have made his "square break". In this connection it is significant to note that in none of his works does Heywood revert to this convention, except in the play of *Wether*, where we have the Vice, Mery Report. For instance, *Witty and Witless* is the theme of a debate, whereas *Wit and Science* in Redford's play are characters, personified abstractions. The style of *Truth and Information* hardly encourages one to think that its author could command the less awkward manner of the *Four PP.*, much less the easy movement of *Gentleness and Nobility*.

> Enformacione emboldyde of the monacorde
> from consonantes to concordes, he musyde hys mastry.
> I assayde the musykes bothe knyght and lorde,
> but none wold speke : the sound-borde was to hy :
> then kept I the playne keys that marde alle my melody ;
> Enformacion drave a crochet that passyde alle my song
> with proporcio parforche dreven on to longe.

He is not always so enigmatic ; the last stanza, the twentieth, ends very happily :

> I kepe be rownd and he be square
> the one ys be mole and the othre be quary
> Yf I myght make tryall, as I cold and dare
> I shold shew why theys ii kyndes do vary ;
> but God knowethe alle ; so doth kyng Hary,
> for yf he dyd, then change sholde thys my song,
> Pyte for pacyens and conscyens for wrong.
> Me nysswhete parabolam f (ecit).
> (Royal, 18. D. 2., f. 163.)

The song is prefaced as follows :

In the Flete maade be me William Cornysshe otherwise called Nysshewhete, Chapelman . . . Henry VII, his reign the XIX yere (1502) the month of July. A treatise betwene Trowth and Enformacion. A.B. of E. how C. for T. was P. in P. (A Ballad of Empson ; how Cornysshe for Treason was Put in Prison.)
(See Edn. Halliwell Phillips.)

This poem does not appear to be at all in the manner of any of the six plays that Dr. Wallace claims for Cornyshe. Its curious and fanciful metaphor is nowhere reflected in them. On the other hand, whatever is curious in Heywood, his verbal repetitions and rhyming vagaries, we find in the

L

CHAPTER VI

THE TWELVE MERRY JESTS OF THE WIDOW EDYTH AND THE HOUSEHOLD OF MORE

Twelve mery gestys of one called Edyth, the lyeing wydow whyche still lyveth. Emprynted at London at the sygne of the mere-mayde at Pollisgate next to chepesyde by J. Rastell, 23 March MDXXV.

IT is a mistake to look upon this entertaining work as belonging to the type of *facetiae* with which Hazlitt published it. It found a place in the third volume of his Shakespeare Jest Books, where its companion pieces are prose collections of miscellaneous anecdotes arranged without plan, after the manner of their prototype, *The Hundred Merry Tales*, which, like the *Wydow Edyth*, was, as we have seen, a production of John Rastell's press. At the time of its publication Walter Smyth, its author, was More's personal servant.

The Widow Edyth was the daughter of a yeoman of Exeter, John Hawkins, whom Herbert, greatly daring, assumed to be the printer of Pynson's edition of Palsgrave's *Lesclarcissement de la langue Francoyse* of 1530. The poem itself disqualifies Herbert's guess.[1] The good Edyth's father married thrice, his third wife, Edyth's mother, burying him after fifteen years of wedded life. Old Hawkins, therefore, did not live to witness his daughter's adventures, which were told in print in 1526, much less did he live to print a book himself in 1530.

---

[1] We might with equal reason accept Swift's ascription of his *Prophecies of Merlin*, imprinted at London by John Haukins in 1533. See Herbert's *Ames*, 470 and 472 n.

His widow, having brought up the child not to

> medle with anything
> that sowned unto good huswyfry
> but aye study to forge and lye,

married her to one Thomas Ellys, and then disappeared
from the story, leaving her daughter a piece of advice that
she did not fail to follow :

> Daughter, make merry, whiles thou may,
> For this world wyll not last alway.

Edyth tired of Thomas and eloped with a servant of the
Earl of Wiltshire, by whom she had a child that died " when
it was but a lad ", and in due time she was " cast up ".
At Andover she told her sorrows to a gentleman to whom
she promised the wardship of a fictitious daughter, a much-
injured heiress. He consulted Sir Thomas Dennis, who
advised him to fetch the girl; but by the time he and the
widow had reached Wandsworth her wiles had become
too apparent, and the first " jest " closes.

From Wandsworth she went to Kew, where the Lord
Chamberlain lay, and there she victimized her poor host
of the house thatched with reed, which she undertook to
replace with a lead roof. Here she won a temporary suitor
in young Thomas, the Lord Chamberlain's barber-surgeon.

> So long they were dallying both day and night,
> Tyll eche had other their trouth yplyght,
> Whiche was the same day, as I hard say,
> That the thatch of the house was pulled away.

The third jest finds her in Suffolk boasting of property
that lay at Thetford, on the strength of which she raises
money and finds free quarters until Mr. Justice Edmund
Lee locks her up for six months in the jail of Bury St.
Edmunds.

Her fourth adventure is one of her most successful. After
deceiving Master Guy and his sister at Stratford-at-Bowe,
she sheltered awhile at Barking Nunnery, but finding

" her profyt did not rest so neare the Nunnes nose ", she repaired to a hostelry at London Stone. Here she proclaimed her determination to forsake worldly wealth and take " the mantle and ring ". She must needs have a confessor, and is recommended to a Doctor of Divinity of the Hospital of St. Thomas of Acre,[1]

> A good publysher of God's word
> In Church and Towne, and sitting at the Bord.

The doctor is almost worthy of a place in the company of Chaucer's " nyne and twentie ".

> She kneeled ther adown on her knees devoutly
> And told her confessour many a great lye.

Moreover, she promised him a scarlet gown and hood and a nest of goblets,

> So that he wolde, while she was in towne,
> Walk with her up and downe,
> And lay out money alway as she neede.

It cost the doctor five nobles, " and then anon she stale away by night ".

Her next victims were Master Frank of Fulham and his wife Annes, who overtook her in distress while they were on their way to offer at the shrine of St. Thomas of Canterbury. She had been robbed and wronged, and was on the point of casting herself into the water. They carried her back to London and entrusted her to a scrivener, Master Rowse. Her property was at Kingston, she said. The scrivener was to make her will. Meanwhile, clad in Mistress Rowse's gown and accompanied by Frank, she made an offering at St. Saviour's, Southwark. But the scrivener had sent to Kingston and learnt the truth, so Edyth was put out that night, by the " back side " " without gown or kyrtle ". As for Master Frank,

> His money was gone and spent indeed
> The blessed Marter quit him his mede.

[1] Afterwards the Mercer's Chapel.

The sixth jest finds the widow in good form. Her property now lay at Windsor, and thither she went, with the servant of a draper who had fitted her out sumptuously. The servant brings back, not money, but a letter referring the good draper to one Master Rowse, scrivener, who will deliver to him a nest of goblets, a dozen spoons, and a standing cup.

> Neiber, quod ye Scriuener, let us drynk some ale
> And speke no more in this matter for shame,
> For ye are begyled and I am the same.

Her next victim was a servant of Sir Thomas Neville, of Tooting :

> She promised hym to be his spouse
> And desired hym to ryde to her house.

She has a daughter under the guardianship of Goodman Ross, of Sevenoaks, who dwells near the church, a carpet-maker. So to Sevenoaks they ride, but when they arrive, she sends him to St. Mary Cray for a casket that lay in her lodging there. He had lent her money and " payed for her cost I cannot tell what ", but there was no widow at " Senock " when he got back.

The household of Bishop Fisher of Rochester provided her with her next dupe, a young serving-man of the episcopal palace.

> She promised him dale and downe
> On that condition he wolde her wed.

He paid her board and kept her company, and their banns were called, but when the Bishop sent for her " to dyne with him and commen [1] further ", " then was she gone ".

Her next attempt was upon the credulity of the Earl of Arundel, who sent five of his serving-men and a maid with her to bring her daughter, the heiress. This adventure ended in the widow being left stripped again of her gown and kirtle by her disillusioned attendants. She lay in hiding for a while next door to Master Heron's, of Foots Cray, and

---

[1] Talk over or discuss the matter.

then, borrowing an outfit from a poor woman, hastened to
Croydon, where she dwelt for a week with a cook, from whom
she borrowed five shillings.

> Then she came to Eltham the right way
> Where she rested her three weekes and a day,
> And did nothyng but ay enquere
> Of gentlemen dwelling here and there.

At length she came to Battersea,

> And on the next day after, she took a whery
> And over Thames she was rowed ful mery.
>
> .   .   .   .   .
>
> At Chelsay was her arivall
> Where she had best cheare of all
> In the house of Syr Thomas More
>
> .   .   .   .   .
>
> At Eltham she sayd that she dyd dwell,
> And of her substance there gan to tell:
> Two wolsted lomes she had, by her fay,
> And two mills that went night and day;
> A Beere brew house, in which every week once
> Twenty quarters were brewed al at once;
> Fowre plowes she kept, the earth to cultiue,
> And xv great knaues to help her to thriue
> Seauen women servants ye wull to spin and carde;
> And to mylke the kyne abroad in the yarde.

There were three young serving-men in the household
at the time who became suitors for the eligible Edyth:
Thomas Croxton, Master Alington's man; Thomas Arthur,
Master Roper's man; and Walter Smyth, the writer of the
book, who was More's personal servant.   Croxton was a
man of great stature, an excellent fellow and Smyth's friend.
Arthur was a man of charming manners and parts, whose
suit had the active support of William Roper and his wife,
Margaret.   Smyth modestly says little of his own endow-
ments.

> Walter Smyth was this young man's name
> One of her louers, and I might tell for shame.

Things went merrily with the widow, and in her chamber

> There was the revell and the gossupping :
> The general bumming, as Marget Giggs sayd.

But Thomas Arthur rode with the widow to recover a debt at Brainford, and there he discovered the truth. Sunday was spent by the widow at Holywell Nunnery where a " sister was that day professed ". Croxton provided groats for the offertory, and Smyth declared his love in the cloister. The rest of the episode, and how the merry Edyth's food and ale are medicated, and other things that ensued, must be left to the reader, who will learn in this tenth jest of the Household of Sir Thomas More things that are not suggested in Roper, but may not be the less true for all that.

> But whether she be content or displeased
> For the space of three weeks ye chaynes she wered
> And after, in a day of a gayle delivery
> She was discharged, being glad and mery.

" Nothing dismaid," she bethought her of My Lord Legate's place, where she asked for a certain knight who, she knew, was away. She told a tale of her wrongs and of her estate to three of Wolsey's yeomen named Shyre, John Clarke, and Thomas ap Richards, all of whom she " bears in hand " before she disappears.

And now we come to the last and longest of the jests. It takes us into the country of John Rastell [1] and the Mores between Barnet and St. Albans, and it is remarkable for the close acquaintance the writer shows with the by-ways and hostelries of the district. The victims are the landlord of the " Three Cups " in Holborn and his man, John Coates. The story is the old one of persecution, of property and wealth lying elsewhere, of money and clothing borrowed, of the discomfiture of mine host of the " Three Cups " and of the widow's escape. There is no meting out of retributive

---

[1] See p. 10.

justice in Smyth's conclusion ; he is too good a disciple of
his master Chaucer to end on the wrong note :

> So " Of these poses I make an ende
> God saue the Wydow, where so euer she wende."

The author of this remarkable little work belonged to a
class from which from the days of Widsith the Scop have
sprung many entertainers and not a few of our writers. He
was a servant in the house of a great man. In 1529, the year
in which he became Lord Chancellor, More obtained for
" Water " [1] Smyth, who had been nine years his personal
servant, the important office of Sword-Bearer to the Lord
Mayor.[2] The ceremonial functions of this office and the
uniform worn on State occasions have changed little. The
Sword-Bearer was the first of the four esquires or gentlemen attendant upon the Lord Mayor,[3] his fellows being the
Common Crier, the Common Hunt, and the Water Bailiff.
In *Roper's Life* there occurs a well-known anecdote of how
the Water Bailiff of London, an old servant of More's, told
his master of scandalous rumours that he had overheard.
As the Water Bailiff at the time appears to have been
Sebastian Hillary, who was from the Royal Household,
I think that an error has occurred in Roper, and that the
reference was to Water Smyth, not to the Water Bailiff.

That Smyth had literary tastes and capacity the poem
shows, but we have remarkable confirmation of this in his
Will : [4]

To John More, his master's only son, he leaves his " Chauscer
of Talles [5] and Boocas." [6]

---

[1] He always spelt his name Water or Waterius, a form of Walter not
uncommon.

[2] Letter Book O, f. 168b, Guildhall.

[3] In the Privy Purse Expenses of Henry VIII, August 1532, occurs the
entry : "Itm the same day paied to one water Smythe for bringing a leshe
of greyhoundes to the kinges grace to Buckingham in rewarde. 7/6." (Ed.
Nicholas, p. 242).

[4] P.C.C. Wills, 8 Cromwell, 1538.

[5] For *Chausceres Talles.*　　　　　　　　　　　　　[6] Boccaccio.

To Clayton's wife, widow of Stephen Puncheon, he leaves his " Englishe Crownicke ".

To the widow of a mercer he leaves his " Englishe Legent ".

To another widow, his " Boke of Bartholome de Proprietatibus Rerum ".

His interest in widows appears to have been persistent, and we must not fail to notice that he left ten shillings for his " fellows " of the Lord Mayor's household, " to drink ".

Although the facts we have recovered are few, yet Walter Smyth emerges from the search a well-defined and interesting figure, a man of mirth, of healthy humour, faithfully attached to More, as all More's protégés were, and rewarded for faithful service by a master who had never neglected the interests of those who had come under his patronage. John Heywood, Dr. John Clement, Richard Hyrde, William Rastell, William Roper, More's secretary (Harris), and Richard Heywood of the King's Bench ; these were all young men who came under the influence of the Chelsea household, and Smyth was More's man from 1520 to 1529, during the time when this influence was most operative.

In fact, the *Merry Jests* and its author yield a very distinct contribution to our knowledge of the More circle. It is good to feel the catholicity of mind and the saving sanity of natural humour that fostered the mingling of piety, scholarship, and unabashed free fun within the More household. It is quite remarkable to find that Berthelet had to explain to the Vicar-General why he had printed without permission Margaret Roper's *Treatise on the Paternoster*,[1] with Richard Hyrde's preface on the *Education of Women*,[2] and yet in the same year Margaret Roper appears in *The Wydow Edyth* as urging the suit of her man, Thomas Arthur, for the widow's hand. Of course, Rastell was not called

[1] Translated from Erasmus. (See Vicar-General's book *Foxford*, described on p. 160.)

[2] Dedicated to Marg. More's young kinswoman, Fraunces S., probably one of Richard Staverton's daughters, a niece of More's (p. 171).

to account for either the *Wydow Edyth* or the *Hundred Merry Tales.*

I believe that not a little of More's hostility to Lutheranism arose out of his conviction of the danger to national sanity of the withering influence of the precisians upon the comic spirit; it would not be surprising to find that he approved of the caution to Berthelet, for we know that William Roper was said to be somewhat Lutheran in his young days. Yet nothing affects the evidence of Smyth's picture of the household; even Margaret Giggs, the scholarly wife of Wolsey's Greek lecturer, joined in the Rabelaisian discomfiture of the widow.

It may seem bold to claim that *The Wydow Edyth* is a narrative of fact, but the author states that this is so, and we shall see that his claim is confirmed by tests.

" This lying widow," he says :

> Late in England hath deceived many
> Both men and women of every degree,
> As wel of the Spiritual as temporaltie
> Lordes, Knightes, and Gentlemen also
> Yeman Groomes, . . .
> Who so lest the matter for to here
> No fayned Stories, but matters in deed
> . . . here may ye reede.

We are, in fact, dealing with actual folk : The Earl of Wiltshire, brother of the Duke of Buckingham ; Sir Thomas Dennis, Sheriff of Devon ; the old Earl of Worcester ; the Lord Chamberlain ; Edmund Lee,[1] Justice of the Peace for Suffolk ; John de Vere, Earl of Oxford ; Sir Thomas Neville, Speaker of the House of Commons ; John Fisher, Bishop of Rochester ; Thomas, Earl of Arundel ; Sir Thomas More ; Wolsey ; these require no investigation. It is when we come to look into the minor characters, the victims themselves, that confirmation becomes most striking. The Subsidy Rolls for 1523–4 for London [2] show that

---

[1] See *Bury Wills* (ed. Sd Tymms), Camden Soc., p. 125, 1535.
[2] R.O., Lay Subsidies, 251/15 B.

our Henry Rowse, scrivener, was assessed at £8 in Chepe
Ward, St. Pancras Parish. The assessment for Wolsey's
household for the same date (Subsidies $\frac{69}{9}$) actually shows
that the three yeomen who were victimized by the widow,
John Clerke, John Shere, and Thomas ap Richards, were
called on to pay a contribution of twelve pence each. Considering how difficult it is to trace even comparatively important people in early Tudor days, this evidence of authen-
ticity will be accepted as remarkable. Then we have
Master Alington, who married Alice Middleton, More's
step-daughter. There is Roper himself who directs in his
will that he shall be buried " in the vawte at Chelsay wt
the body of my dearelie beloved wief (whose soule oure Lord
pardon) where my father in-lawe Sir Thomas More (whose
sowle Jesus blesse) did mynd to be buried ". Master Heron,
of Foots Cray, may also have been of the More circle, for the
Chancellor's daughter Ciceley married Giles Heron. Nor may
we omit Margaret Giggs. Of the characters actually named
in *The Wydow Edyth*, I have traced all but the widow's father
John Hawkins, her husband Thomas Ellys, Master Guy
and his sister of Stratford, John Frank and his wife of
Fulham, Goodman Rosse of Sevenoaks, the two servants of
Roper and Alington, and John Coates of Holborn. There
is no doubt, however, that these are all equally real people,
and we need not despair of tracing them. Similarly, the
itinerary of the widow bears scrutiny. The story opens at
Exeter in the household of old John Hawkins of the " Fleur
de Lys." It moves to Andover, thence to Wandsworth,
and so on to Kew. We next find the widow at Horinger
Heath, near Bury St. Edmunds ; thence she goes to Brandon-
ferry and Bradfolde, and after a second visit to the gaol
at Bury, she moves to Earls Colne in Essex, and so to Stratford at Bowe. From Barking she comes to London, where
she beguiles the Doctor of Divinity, the scrivener Rowse,
the Franks of Fulham, and the anonymous draper. And
then in merry chase we follow her to Tooting, Sevenoaks,

CHAPTER VII

THE REGULATION OF THE BOOK TRADE BEFORE
THE PROCLAMATION OF 1538

IN dating the More circle plays (*Four PP.*, *Pardoner and Frere*, and *Johan Johan*) account must be taken of the definite change that took place about the year 1525 in the ecclesiastical atmosphere. It is safe to say that they must have been written in days that were care-free though critical, before the religious machinery which they ridicule had become the target of the Lutherans. They belong to an earlier phase exemplified in the *Encomium Moriae* of Erasmus, or More's letter on the Coventry friar. The evidence which I propose to set out in this chapter shows that this change of atmosphere may be dated with some definiteness. It has interest also for the light it throws on the publication of Margaret Roper's little treatise in the same year in which Walter Smyth's *XII Merry Jests* took the light. Further, it explains the circumstances in which More found it to be his duty to undertake the heavy task of his controversial work.

Richard Foxford, Vicar-General of the Bishop of London, gave his name to the first volume of the Consistorial records known as the Vicar-General's Books. *Foxford* covers the years 1520–38, and its contents are of the most miscellaneous character. In it we find wills, administrations, advowsons, presentations, sequestrations, and examinations as to abuses of pluralities ; it records marriage licences, licences to consecrate, to preach, to collect alms, to exercise the art of surgery, and to practise midwifery. Among the marriage licences are those of the three daughters of Sir Thomas More. It records the profession of an " Ankeresse " and the tragic death of a bellringer who was carried up on his rope, and it contains a large number of cases of clerical misdemeanours, amongst which is one of a curate who used a love charm which I am unable to decodify.   Hidden away in this confusion of matter, all in ecclesiastical law Latin, ill-written and much abbreviated, we find between the years 1524 and 1528 five records touching the regulation of the London book trade.

The importance of the five cases rests on the fact that they carry us back to an earlier stage in the history of the regulation of the English trade than it has been possible hitherto to investigate.   They show us in working the methods of the diocesan and ecclesiastical control that preceded that by the King and Privy Council, which may be said to have begun with the Royal Proclamation of 1529 and under which the Stationers' Company some twenty-six years later was to receive its Charter.   The five cases illustrate the closing stages of this diocesan and ecclesiastical regulation.   They show us the procedure of a system that had been set up originally to deal with Lollardy and was now being applied unsuccessfully to the problems of the Lutheran heresy.

This system seems to have been sanctioned by an Act of Parliament of 1410 known as the Statute " Ex Officio " in which were embodied the main provisions of the Provincial Constitutions drawn up under Archbishop Arundel at a Synod at Oxford in 1407.   The terms of the Statute which apply to books are as follows :

That none hereafter do—make or write any book contrary to the catholic faith and determination of the Holy Church— and further that no man hereafter shall by any means favour —any such book maker or writer—and that all persons having any of the said books writings or schedules containing the said wicked doctrines and opinions shall within 40 days deliver them to the ordinary of the same place.   And if any person do attempt any manner of thing contrary to the statute then the ordinary of the same place, in his own diocese by authority of

M

the same proclamation and Statute shall cause to be arrested and detained under safe custody the said person in this case defamed and evidently suspected. And that the said ordinary, by himself, or his Commissaries, proceed openly and judicially to all the effect of law against the said persons so arrested.

Thus it lay with the Bishop and his officials to deal by legal and open trial in the diocesan courts with the makers and writers of heretical books. This statute, however, which gave sanction to the legal proceedings that we shall presently consider was preceded and led up to by Arundel's *Provincial Constitutions*, two of which, Constitutions VI and VII, also deal with books.

Constitution VI provides for a censorship of books read at the Universities and elsewhere in schools, halls and hostels. The censors were to be appointed by the Universities subject to the discretion of the Archbishop, and their verdict of approval was expressly to be confirmed by him before the book was handed to the Stationer to be copied. Thus the Archbishop controlled the censorship of such books as were likely to propagate error, namely those that were " read ", as we still say, at the Universities.

Constitution VII forbids the translation of the Scriptures and the reading of any such " book, libel, or treatise— set forth in the time of John Wyclif or since, or hereafter to be set out ".

In his *Dialogue* of 1528 More refers to this Constitution as sanctioning the action then recently taken against Tyndale's translation.

The machinery of this system was designed to check the dissemination of heresy in the days before printing, and it is natural that the first methods adopted to meet the Lutherans should follow the lines laid down for the frustration of the Lollards.

Before I pass on, however, to the Lutheran period, I would draw attention to the existence of a pre-Lutheran Episcopal licence for a printed book issued in 1514 by the Bishop of London for a devotional work by one " wretched Symon, the anker of London Wall ". The colophon of Symon's *Treatise* is as follows :

Here endeth the Treatyse called the Fruyte of Redemption, whiche devoute Treatyse I Rycharde unworthy Bysschop of London have studyously radde and overseen, and the same approve as moche as in me is to be radde of the true Servantes of Swete Jhesu, to theyr grete Consolacyon and ghostly Comforte and to the meryte of the devoute Fader Compounder of the same. Emprynted by Wynkyn de Worde, the yere of our Lord God MCCCCC and XIIII.

If Rychard FitzJames, Bishop of London, had written an Introduction to "wretched" Symon's lucubrations he could not have done it more kindly. Moreover, it was not the act of an "unleisured licenser" or of a board of scrutineers. But things were about to suffer a rude change, how rude we may judge by comparing the colophon I have just quoted with the end of John Gough's *Dore of Holy Scripture* in 1540.

Perused by doctor Tayler and doctor Barons
Master Coton and Master Torner.

If we may judge by his will,[1] John Gough was another veritable "wretched Symon ", but he was denied the satisfaction of feeling that an imprimatur was a pat on the back.

FitzJames, however, was an aged man, and he belonged to a bygone day that liked anchorites but feared the New Learning. He was too old or too narrow to appreciate the liberalism of his Dean, John Colet, whom he would have made a heretic, said Tyndale, for translating the *Paternoster* into English, had not Warham helped him. The old times were passing rapidly, and though it fell to Tunstall, his successor, to bear the brunt of the battle, FitzJames lived long enough to see the opening of the great Lutheran struggle.

The call to action against the new heresy and its propagation by means of the printing press came in the

---

[1] *Comm. of Lond. Wills*, Storey, 25th September, 1542.

that these were newly composed and made, they were not to sell or part with them unless first they showed them either to the Lord Cardinal, the Archbishop of Canterbury, the Bishop of London or the Bishop of Rochester.

Then follow the names of Nicholas Sutton and Thomas Kellys, a space being left for the names of the other book-sellers, which unfortunately were not written in. The monition, it will be noted, says nothing of the licensing of books produced at home. Apparently no danger was apprehended from England that was not already adequately provided for. It lays down the law that Lutheran books produced abroad must be licensed.

The channels, however, through which imported books circulated ran underground, and the cases of offence against Tunstall's monition that came up before the Vicar-General were not of a very mischievous kind.

On 19th October, 1525, Wynkyn de Worde and John Gough were summoned to answer the charge of having published a translation made by Gough called *The Image of Love.*

II. The Case of the Vicar-General against Wynkyn de Worde, Printer.

On 19th December, 1525, in St. Paul's Cathedral before Master Wharton, assisted by Master John Olyuer there appeared the aforesaid Winandus who confessed that he was present when the Bishop of London enjoined and warned him and the other printers as is contained in the acts above ; and further he confessed that since the aforesaid monition he had printed a certain work in the vulgar tongue called *The Image of Love,* alleged to contain heresy, of which he said he sent sixty to the Nuns of Syon, and as many more he sold. John Gough, Printer, likewise of the City also appeared and confessed that he had translated the said book or work for the said Winandus to print, which he received, so he said, from a certain Edward Lockwood of the Parish of St. Brides ; and then the Vicar-General warned them that if they had any of these books to sell not to sell or part with them, and that they should get back those already sold and have them brought in before Christmas ; and that they should also have copies of this work that had been sold or sent to the Universities of Cambridge or Oxford, brought in before the Feast of the Epiphany ; further he warned them to appear before him in Consistory on the third day after St. Hilary to reply to articles concerning suspicion of heresy, in the presence of Master Henry Hyckman and Dominus Robert Lay.

The offending book, *The Image of Love*, is described in a spirit of admiration in More's *Dialogue* (by the Messenger, who, it may be pointed out, plays the part of devil's advocate). To the Messenger, *The Image of Love*

seemed to be the work of some very virtuous man contemplative and well lerned. The good holy man layeth sore against these carved and painted Ymages . . . specially leste commendyng such as be most costely, curyously and most workemanly wrought. And he sheweth full well that ymages be but laymens bookes, and therefore that religious men . . . should let all such dede ymages passe and labour onely for the lyvely quicke ymage of love . . . In the time (of the Saintes of olde) thei had treen chalices and golden prestes and now have we golden chalices and treen prestes.—(*Workes*, p. 114.)

These were dangerous opinions with which to indoctrinate the nuns of Syon, and they savour not a little of the new precisian spirit. Therefore the printer and translator were " troubled ", as Foxe would say, in the Bishop's court to answer to articles concerning suspicion of heresy ; but of what happened to them on 15th January there is no record in *Foxford*.

The librarian of Stonyhurst College has very kindly described for me the copy of the *Ymage of Love* in the College Library. It has no reference to the translator, so that we may claim to have learnt for the first time from *Foxford* that the English is the rendering of Gough. More did not know who was the author of the work. The date is given in the sermon made by the Bishop in his own writing or at least subscribed by him. He also printed another work by Erasmus called *Immensa Misericordia Dei*, translated into English by Jensian Harbart, a layman of the household of the Countess of Salisbury, as well as another work called the *Sayings of the Wise*, translated from the Latin into English by the respondent himself. Questioned then as to whether he showed or exhibited the said works to the Lord Cardinal, the Archbishop, or the Bishops of London or Rochester according to the requirements of the acts recorded above, he replied that he had not. And then the Vicar-General enjoined him that he should not hereafter sell any copies of the above works, and that he should not print any works without first exhibiting them before him in Consistory; and he warned him to appear on the third day after the feast of St. Monica to see further.

The three works of Erasmus, *The Paternoster*, *The Immense Mercy* and the *Dicta Sapientium* would certainly not have been forbidden by his friends, Tunstall, Fisher and Warham, although controversialists like Lee of York had troubled Erasmus by their attacks on his New Testament. As for Fisher's sermon, it was the one preached at Paul's Cross against Luther on the wet day in February.

Berthelet's fault, then, was a technical one : he had neglected to exhibit his copy ; and the case points to a tightening of the hold which the Bishop's officials had put upon the printers.

Further, it is clear that the Court exercised the wider powers that it possessed, as I have suggested under the Constitutions of 1409, and that it was not limited by the terms of Tunstall's inhibition of 12th October, which dealt only with imported books. One of the works mentioned in this case is of more than ordinary interest, namely Margaret Roper's translation of Erasmus' *Treatise on the Paternoster*, and that quite independently of its importance as the work of More's daughter, done when she was only nine-

teen. The value of the book is greatly enhanced by the
introduction contributed to it by a young scholar, Richard
Hyrde, a tutor in the Chelsea household. This introduction,
as Dr. Foster Watson has pointed out in his reprint of it in
Vives and the Renaissance Education of Women, is the first
modern English work on female education. It vindicates
their right to inclusion in the circle of the humanists of the
New Learning. Hyrde dedicated his introduction to his
pupil, " the most studyous and virtuous yonge mayde
Fraunces S.", who, we learn from her tutor, was kinswoman
to Margaret and was being educated in the household of her
uncle (More). But by a strange mishap, due to his desire to
connect this document with Ascham's well-known eulogy
of another " virtuous young maid ", Lady Jane Gray, Dr.
Watson assumes that the Frances S. is Frances Brandon,
daughter of the Duke of Suffolk, mother of Lady Jane ;
and thus Henry VIII usurps the place of More as uncle.
In this way he reaches a conclusion that I am loath to
disturb when he writes : " This Introduction thus is connected
with some of the most important women's names of the
period—the More household ; Henry VIII's household,
including Catherine of Aragon and her daughter Mary ;
the Queen Widow Mary, her daughter Frances, and grand-
daughter Lady Jane Grey ".

A young scholar of More's household would hardly address
a princess of the blood as Frances S. and " mine own good
gentle and fair Fraunces ", and I suppose that Hyrde was
addressing someone much nearer to his affections than
Frances Brandon, namely a niece of More's and daughter of
More's brother-in-law, Richard Staverton, Attorney of the
Guildhall. We are not allowed, however, to follow out the
romance of Richard Hyrde and Frances S. to a happy ending,
because in 1528, when Hyrde accompanied Gardiner and
Foxe to Italy as secretary and physician on an Embassy
to the Pope, the party were overtaken by storm and had to
ford a river in spate ; Hyrde caught a chill and died, to the
great grief of Gardiner and Foxe, who have left a record of
their sense of loss in a letter to Wolsey.

Edward Isengold	Henry Pepwell	Robertus Redman
Thomas Kellyt	William Bonam	Ricus Banks
Wynkyn de Worde	Simon Coston	Johnes Collyns
Arnold	Ricus Falkes	Robert Copland
Cowerd	Thomas Petyt	Nich^{as} Sutton
Mestres Andrew	Michaell	Johnes Scott
Henricus Hermon	Henr^{us} Dabb	Robertus Wyer
Johnes Rowse	Johnes Groot	Thomas Bartlett
Lodowic Sutton	Johes Toye	Johnes Reyns
Johnes Heron	Johes Gowghe	Mr. Rastell
	Ricus Pynson	

This inhibition is much more comprehensive than the earlier one in that it definitely brings under the control of the ecclesiastical licensers the printing and sale in London of all books not hitherto approved, whether of English or foreign origin.

The list of booksellers is, of course, valuable and interesting, and one only regrets the absence of a similar list in the Monition of 1524. It is to be noted, however, that there is no evidence that the members of the book trade were treated as Members of the Stationers' Company. We happen to know from Letter Book O of the Corporation Records that the Wardens of the Stationers' Company on 9th October, 1526, that is a fortnight earlier than this schedule, were Henry Pepwell and Lewis Sutton. These names are, however, in no way distinguished in our present list, the one occurring ninth, the other eleventh in the thirty-one names. It will be noticed that there was one woman present, Mestres Andrew, perhaps the mother or aunt of Laurence Andrew, who ran away owing £20 to John Rastell for printing stuff, and left his aunt to settle the matter. It may also be noted that Rastell, who prosecuted the aunt, is distinguished as Master Rastell, being a lawyer, and that he has an added dignity from his position at the foot of the bill.

There is only one recorded prosecution under the new monition, and it occurred almost a year afterwards.

V. The Case of the Vicar-General against Robert
Wyer, Printer.

On the same day (7th September, 1527) there appeared
before Mr. Wharton, Vicar-General, in St. Paul's Cathedral,
Robert Wyer, Printer, who confessed that he had been
warned by the Bishop of London that he should not print
any work, particularly of Holy Writ, nor sell the same
under the penalty contained in the monition, and that
since the monition in contempt of the same (*in ridiculum
eiusdem*), he had caused to be translated into the vulgar
tongue *Symbolum Apostolicum*, containing many errors and
that he also printed it, and the Vicar-General warned him
under pain of suspicion of heresy to appear before him on
the following Monday to exhibit all and every such book
remaining in his possession, and that he should do his
diligence to return to the Vicar-General the rest sold by him.
He appeared on the following Monday and exhibited in the
presence of the Vicar-General, twenty-nine books containing
the said *Symbolum* which he left at the Registry and the
Vicar-General appointed that he should appear before the
Bishop of London after his arrival in England to hear
his will upon the premises.

I have not been able to trace Wyer's *Symbolum Apostolicum*. The Treatise by Erasmus on the Apostles' Creed,
written for Thomas, Earl of Wiltshire, bears a later date
(1533) in the preface. Further there may be doubt as to the
meaning of *in ridiculum eiusdem*. Does it mean that
Wyer published a parody, or simply that he had acted
contemptuously in disregarding the demands of the monition ? I think it bears the latter meaning, for, if it had been
a work intended to raise laughter, the court would not have
described it as translated and " containing many errors ".

Wyer's is the last of the five cases recorded in *Foxford*,
and so far as I have examined it there are no further
references to booksellers in the Vicar-General's books.
Wolsey's days of power were drawing to a close. His methods

elliswhere printyd of them sell wythin thys realme duryng
the space of VII yeres next after this furst impression ".

Pynson's first three privileged books appear to be :

1. A *Sermon* by Pace printed in November, 1518, "cum
privilegio a rege indulto ne quis hanc orationem intra biennium
. . . imprimat ".

2. *A Sermon in praise of Matrimony* by Tunstall of the same
month and year bearing the same imprint.

3. Wm. Horman's *Vulgaria* in 1519 with a colophon " . . .
cum privilegio . . . ne quis haec imprimat nec aliubi impressa,
importataque intra regnum Anglix vendat ".

We cannot be sure that these three early privileges of
Pynson's are authors' privileges, but they are for single
books. After this both Pynson and Rastell issued their
books under a general privilege, using the phrase *cum
privilegio a rege indulto* or its equivalent, without any
reference to the particular work in hand.

I therefore conclude that the first privileges were for
individual books or grants of copyright to authors and that
in certain cases like Palsgrave's in 1530 such privileges
continued to be granted, but that about the years 1519–20
John Rastell and Richard Pynson were relieved of the
necessity of seeking a licence of protection for separate works
by the grant of a general privilege. I would add that
as Wynkyn de Worde, Julian Notary, Richard Faques,
Robert Copland, Henry Pepwell, John Skot and Peter
Treveris do not appear to have had privileges, it would seem
that Pynson and Rastell were the first English printers to
enjoy royal protection of this kind.

They were joined, it appears, in 1525 by Robert Redman,
and in 1526 Thomas Berthelet, and after that the younger
men, troubled by the atmosphere of suspicion under which
they worked, found it advisable to seek the royal protection.
For, after all, it was a mark of respectability, even though it
left them subject to the censor. Thus Thomas Godfray,
Robert Wyer, Richard Banks, Laurence Andrewe, Wm.
Rastell, John Byddell, Thomas Gibson, John Gough, Thomas

Petyt, John Wayland, John Mayler, Wm. Middleton, John Herforde, Thomas Raynalde, Richard Lant, William Bonham, and of course Grafton and Whitchurch all used the King's privilege. Yet an old hand like de Worde went along unprotected except in the vicarious cases in which he was printing for some one else who had the privilege.

We may notice, however, before we leave the question of the two kinds of privilege, that the monopolies, sometimes lucrative, for classes of books which were granted later, whether for grammars, Bibles and service books or law books, even if we look on them as a development of the privilege at first granted to authors like Linacre, Palsgrave, Whitinton and Rastell, really formed a class apart, and were a special concession granted under letters patent. On the other hand, it is worth notice that no original warrant or licence has been found, so far as I know, granting a general privilege to a printer, although copies of these warrants are sometimes printed in full in their books after 1538.

The rapid development of the practice of granting general privileges after 1525 may be associated, as I have suggested, with the atmosphere of suspicion under which printers were working. In any case it is clear that the words *cum privilegio regis* would give confidence to the poor reader, who must have been almost afraid to buy a book lest he might find himself arraigned before the Bishop's Court. On the other hand, hardened controversialists like Bale resented the appearance of " popish " books under the King's privilege. In his *Yet a Course at the Romysh Fox* he attacked Richard Lant for printing *cum privilegio*, a work that annoyed him, and sought comfort in declaring that " he hath dyshonoured hys kinge and dishonested his cuntre in offering (it) unto the peple under his tyttle of privylege ".

Bale was not using a new controversial weapon, for I have found a delightful case [1] of its use for defence in 1534, that must have opened the eyes of the King if he ever heard of it. The village of Langham, in Essex, had evidently a

[1] R.O., Misc. Bks., T.R., 120, p. 59.

fair copy,[1] then submitted to the King with the final corrections in his own royal hand. I am therefore able to state that the words *ad imprimendum solum* were the addition of Henry VIII himself. The series of drafts and emendations are so interesting, however, that I will go through them in order, and I do this the more readily because they confirm Mr. Pollard's reading of the King's phrase in a definite manner. The first draft reads :

item that no person or persons usyng the occupacion of pryntyng in this Realme shall from henceforth prynte any boke in the Englishe tong with theise wordes, (cum privilegis Regali) onless the true understonding of the same wordes be plainlie declard and expressed in the Englshe tong underneth them to the intent that the Reders may plainlie perceve the effecte therof.

This draft is important as showing that the original scope of the injunction was confined to the use and abuse of the phrase *cum privilegio regali* and their effect on readers.

It was then felt that this was insufficient, for the point needed emphasis that the privilege was not an imprimatur. Hence we get the first correction of the first draft.

item that no person or persons usyng the occupacion of pryntyng in this Realme shall from henc-forth prynte eny boke in the Englishe tong with theise wordes (cum privilegio Regali) onless they have first licence of his higness graunted upon examinacion made by some of his graces privy counsaill to printe the same. And have a privilege in dede that no man but they shall printe the same for a tyme plainly declard and expressed in the Englishe tong underneth them to the extent that the Reders may plainlie perceve the effecte thereof.

In many ways this is a satisfactory version. It states what a privilege is, namely, a grant " that no man but they shall printe the book for a tyme " ; it demands that the printer who uses it shall have it " in dede " which means, of course, that some poor beggars of printers were rascally enough to

[1] B.M., Cott. Cleop. E.V., 341.

filch the words ; and it distinguishes the King's privilege
from the censor's licence or imprimatur.

The next version or correction relieved the Privy Council
of the direct responsibility of being the only duly empanelled
licensing authority by adding to their number " such other
as his hignes shal appointe ", and it cleared up the two
questions of the filching of the *cum privilegio* and the
interpretation of the words to the reader by a clever stroke.
The printer was to print " theffecte " of both his licence and
his privilege plainly in English. If he had never had such a
licence and a privilege granted to him, he could not state
their " effect ", and if he stated their effect, readers could
have no ground for misunderstanding their plain object.

The second correction then reads :

item that no person or persons usyng the occupacion of
pryntyng in this Realme shall from henc-forth prynte eny boke
in the Englishe tong with theise words / cum privilegio Regali /
onless they have firste licence of his higness graunted upon
examinacions made by some of his graces privy counsaill or
other such as his highnes shal appointe And that theeffecte
of his licence and privilege be thereto prynted and plainlie
declared and expressed in the English tong underneth them.

So far we have followed the Record Office draft. A fair
copy was now made with only one slight change, stiffening
the last phrase,

and that the hole copie or els at the least the effect of his
licence and privilege.

and this fair copy was submitted to the King, who amended
it very definitely in his own hand. This copy with the
King's corrections is in Cotton MS. Cleopatra E.V. at the
British Museum.

His Majesty was evidently the first to see that the injunction so far applied only to those who used the words *cum
privilegio regàli,* and that its effect would be to leave all
other printers free of the injunction. He also detected that
the words " using the occupation of pryntyng " were not

wanted, since without them the phrase ran " no person or persons in this realme ". As for all this to-do about the distinction between a licence and a privilege, let them add to the words *cum privilegio regali* the words *ad imprimendum solum*, " for printing only ", or as an earlier draft had put it, " that no man but they shall printe the same for a tyme ", and there was an end of it. So the final state of the copy, the state in which it went to Berthelet after the King's handling, ran

Item that no person or persons in this realm shall from henceforth printe any booke in the Englishe tong unless upon examination made by some of his Grace's pryvie counsaille or other such as His Highnesse shall appoint they shall have lycence so to do and yet so havynge nott to put these words Cum privilegio regali without addyng Ad imprimendum solum, and that the hole copie, or els at the least theeffect of his licence and privilege be therwith printed, and playnely declared and expressed in the Englisshe tonge underneth them.

In accordance with the injunction as it thus finally appeared in the proclamation of 1538, books now began to appear containing a copy of the privilege granted by the King. We find this, for instance, in Berthelet's edition of Sir Thomas Elyot's *Dictionary* of 1538, in John Gough's *Dore of Holy Scripture* of 1540, and Richard Banks' *Epistles and Gospels* of the same year. Gough was on more than one occasion in trouble with the authorities, and his privilege is made conditional upon his " Storyes or bokes being perused and overseen by two or three dyscrete learned persons " ; but such a condition was apparently unusual, and it is not stated either in Berthelet's or Banks' privilege.

The following copy of Richard Banks' privilege will illustrate the nature of these grants :

Henry the eight by the grace of god kynge of Englande etc. To all prynters of bokes wythin thys oure Realme and to all other our officers ministers and subiectes, these our letters hearyng or seynge, gretyng. We let you wit that of our grace especial, we have gyven privilege unto our welbeloved subiecte Richarde Bankes, that no maner person wythin thys our realme, shal prynte any maner of bokes what so ever our sayd subiecte shall prynte fyrste wythin the space of seven yeres next ensuying the prentynge of every suche boke so by hym prynted, upon payne of forfeting the same.   Wherefore we woll and comaunde you, that ye nor none of you, do presume to prynte any of the sayde bokes durynge the tyme aforesayde as ye tender oure pleasure, and woll avoyde the contrarye.

I have pointed out earlier that in Gough's *Dore of Holy Scripture* the licence as well as the privilege was printed :

Perused by doctor Taylor, and doctor Barons, Master Ceton and Master Torner.

We have already noticed that no original grant or warrant of privilege has been found.   The reason for this would appear to be that, being neither a warrant for payment nor receipt it was not filed for reference by the auditors or tellers.   In that it differed, for instance, from the enrolled letters patent that record a grant of a pension.   A letter to Cromwell from Hilsey, Bishop of Rochester, compiler of the Primer, shows, however, how a privilege might be published.   " May it please you^r Lordeshippe," he writes, " to declare unto this berer the prynter, the pryvylege y^t he shall obteyn by you^r Lordshippe favorable kyndness—Certyfienge hym further wyther yt may please yor Lordeshippe that the comandement to the rest of the prynters shalbe declarede unto them by yor messenger other els prynted in the prymer."

In the year 1538, when the King's new phrase *ad imprimendum solum* became compulsory, Grafton was in Paris engaged on his Great Bible.   He had finished the New Testament and had used the old phrase *cum gratia et privilegio regis* when Lord Hertford informed him of the new inhibition.   He at once wrote to Cromwell in distress about the added words " which wordes we never heard of before neither do we take it that these wordes shoulde be added in the pryntyng of the Scripture (yf yt be truely translated) for then shuld yt be a great occasyon to the enemys to say that yt is not the Kynges acte or mynde

to set yt forth, but only lycence the prynters to sell soche as
is put forth " ; a legitimate criticism, all will agree, but one
that shows a clear apprehension of the meaning of the
King's phrase.

Whatever trouble these words may have given, I would
venture to point out that we ought at least to be grateful
to Henry VIII for affording us a clear and irrefragable piece
of evidence as to the backward date of all books that
bear the imprint *ad imprimendum solum.* No one ever
dreamt of using these words in an imprint before the King
himself inserted them into a copy of the proclamation in
1538. Further, we should be grateful to Grafton for the
evidence he has left us of the meaning the phrase had for a
printer in 1538. Any other meaning than " for printing
only " makes nonsense of his letter to Cromwell, whatever
uses the phrase was put to in later days.[1]

If, as we leave the little plot that we have been surveying,
we were to ask what we had found there our answer might
be that we had seen how Wolsey, the Papal Legate, tried to
enforce the injunction of Leo X touching heretical books,
and how it fell to the Bishop of London to control the London printers ; that we had seen his Consistorial Court at
work and had found that it is really very true that new wine
is too much for old bottles. We had seen that when the
Vicar-General had troubled the printers, the Royal Privilege began to find favour in the eyes of the younger men.
We had seen that some printers abused the privilege and
others who had never received it falsely claimed to have it.
We had seen that readers affected to think that they too were
protected by it. We had seen finally how the King and the
Privy Council took over the control of the book trade and
how Henry himself brushed aside the privilege dispute and
had his Privilege defined.

A discussion of the phrase *Ad imp. sol.* by Miss E. M. Albright appeared
in *Mod. Lang. Notes,* February 1919, and by Mr. A. W. Pollard in *The
Library,* January 1919.

THE LAW OF NATURE

RASTELL: APPENDIX I

JOHN RASTELL'S VOYAGE IN THE YEAR 1517

But they that were the venturers
Have cause to curse their maryners
Fals of promys and dissemblers
That falsly them betrayed.
—Rastell's *Play of The Four Elements.*

THAT a voyage had been attempted in or about the year 1517 is indicated by a passage in Eden's dedicatory preface to Münster's *Cosmographie* (1553), when he says that to meet death in such attempts is more honourable than to die in soft beds at home among the tears of women. " Whiche manlye courage, yf it had not been wanting in other in these our dayes, at suche time as our soveryin Lord of noble memori King Henry the VIII about the same yere of his raygne (*Anno VIII* = 1516–17) furnished and sent forth certen shippes under the governaunce of Sebastian Cabot yet living and one Sir Thomas Perte (*sic*) whose faynt heart was the cause that the viage took none effect. . . ."

Sir Thomas Sperte was signing indentures on 10th July, 1517, with the Lord Admiral, Thomas, Earl of Surrey, on his appointment to the office of " balastyng of shippes in the Thames "[1]; but as I read the case, I see no need to correct Eden's reference, although it is obvious that Surrey himself was opposed to sending any part of his fleet across the Atlantic when it might be needed in the Channel.[2] Sperte, Master of the *Henri Grace à Dieu*, was one of Henry's leading master mariners. The several mutinous mariners, who are mentioned in the law-suit, and the vessels, the *Barbara* and *Mary Barking*, are frequently met with in the naval records of the period. Cabot, however, I believe to have been innocent, and he is not referred to in the

[1] R.O., A/cs. Excheqr Q.R., 57. 17.
[2] This in spite of the fact that Surrey may have been one of Rastell's sureties.

wel to all yor subjects as to all other crestyn princes and theyr
subjects for the fortherance of the same. And for the same
viage yor seyd orator reteynyd in his service John Ravyn to
be purser of a shypp called ye barbara. Which seyd ravyn
contrarye to ye trust ye he was put in and contrarye to all
trewthe deseyved yor seyd orator causyd and compelyd hym
to gyff up his viage to his gret losse and forthermore after y^t
yor seyd orator had thus by compulsyon gyffyn up his viage,
the seyd ravyn cam to the seyd shypp at falmouth / and ther
he and dyvers of the false mareners that is to say Edward taylor,
John brian, humfrey dyke servants to the seid Ravyn wt many
mo of the lyke felons and robbers put out of the seyd shipp one
Rychard Walker y^t was servant and factor to yo seyd orator
and there spoyled & toke away ye goodes of y^r seyd orator
beying in ye sayd shypp y^t ys to sey / fyne white flowre and
bay salt wt certeyn pakks of frysis and canvas and cofers of
silks and tukes and other mercery ware wt divers other goodes
and howsold stuff / as fedyr bedes napery pannes pottes and
dyvers other wares as salt / hiddes tallow and other thynges
as shall appere by percelles which goodes amount to ye some
off C pounds and above whereof yor seyd orator had nei(ther)
rekonyng nor recompence unto this day to ye valew of one
peny /

And now so it is that ye seyd ravyn w^t many other of the
seyd malefactors be now abydyng w^t -in the cyte of london
pleasyth it yor gracious hyghnes ye premissis tenderly consideryd/
as to send one or yor offyce^{rs} of ye seriauntes of armes or some
other offycer of yor s to attach ye seyd personnes to appere
before yor grace and yor honorable counsell and there to make
answere of theyr misdemean^{rs} and robbery and to fynd suerti
to make recompence to yor orato^r of all y^t yor grace or yor
honorable counsell shall there by ye law resonably adiugge.
As yor seyd orato^r shal dayly pray for ye prosperous estate of
your gracious hyghnes.

II. *The answer of John Ravyn to the bill of complaynt of
John Rastell.*

The saide John Ravyn seyth that the saide bill is untrue
uncerteyn and unsufficient to be answered to and feyned of
malice to thentent to put the saide John Ravyn to expences
and trouble and the matter therin conteyned matter clerly
determynable parti at the comyn lawe and parte before thadmyrall
of the See and not in this honourable Courte / wherunto he preyth

to be remytted / And thadvauntage therof to hym savid / if he be compelled to make ferther answer to the saide insufficient bill.

Ferther that as to the saide disseyt compulsion or lettyng of the saide John Rastell of his saide viage takyng or spoilyng of any man^r of goodes or wares or any other myssdemeano^r in the saide feyned bill submytted that he is not therof ne of noo parte therof gyltie in manner and fourme as the saide John Rastell bi his saide bill hath surmytted / all whiche matters the saide John Ravyn is redy to prove as this honourable Court shall awarde / and pryth to be dysmyssed oute of the same with his reasonable coste systeyned in this behailfe accordyng to the statutes in suche case provided.

III. *The replicacon of John Rastell to the answere of John Ravyn.*

The seyd John Rastell seyth that his seyd bill is good and trew in every poynt and nothyng faynyd and that the seyd John Ravyn is gylty in every poynt and article as is alegyd in the seyd byll whych the seyd John Rastell is redy to prove accordyng to the order of thys court / and for as much as the seyd John Ravyn hath so spoylyd and takyn away the goodes of the seyd John Rastell so that for lack of possession of his seyd goodes he is not able to maynteyn and sew the comyn law wherfor he prayeth that the seyd Ravyn may be compellyd to put in sewrte to restore the seyd goodes and damage for w^t holdyng of the same as it shall be by this honorable court resonably aduigged.

IV. *Interrogatoryes in the matter between John Rastell and John Ravyn.*

The furst article.

In Primis Whether John Ravyn was deseyvable and negligent in doyng service to the seyd J Rastell and whether he was absent when the ship called the Barbara whereof he was reteyned to be purser dept^d to Gravesend / wher the ship taryed for hym when other shippes of the same fleet departed by reason wherof that ship was set aground on the hornys lyke to be lost when the seyd J Rastell tarryed for them at Sandwych and other shippes of the same flete departed. Richard Walker sworn and examined upon this interrogatory saith upon his othe that the forsaid shipe and company in hyr taried for the said Ravyn the space of ij dayes by reason wherof she was ne^r loste but what cause or occasion she had so to tary this deponent knowt not.

and alowyd himself money for them / whych Raster was seke of the agew before he cam abord and so contynewyd and dyd never servyce / and also toke and alowyd himself money after the rate off VIs. a monyth for one humfrey dyke his servant to be a gunner which coud nothyr skyll to be a marener nor gonner this article the said Walker sayth ys true but whether it needed any moo mareners to be had for that viage this deponent cannot depose.

the VIIth.

Also whethyr that Richard Walker whom Rastell had deputyd his factor to bordews proclaymyd in the country at falmouth that he wold sell the salt the goodes of Rastell / and when the people cam thedyr to by hit one Edward Taylor Humfrey dyke and other mareners there dy^d mete the salt themself and sold it and reseyved the money both for the salt that was the goodes of rastell and also the salt that was the goods of one Richard Spicer in the same ship contrary to the mynde of Richard Walker, (and) contrary to the mynd of Richard Mylward then factor ther to the seyd Spicer the said Walker confesseth upon his othe that this article ys true.

the VIIIth.

Also whether Richard Walker came to my lord of Surrey at blechyng lee desyryng hym to be good lord to the seyd Rastell shewyng hym how yvyll the mareners had intretyd hym whych seyd that he had send down John Ravyn to take the ship unto his own hand and commandyd Walker that he shuld no more meddyll wt Rastells goodes beyng in the shep and seyd that ravyn knew forther of hys mynd also the said Walker sayth this article ys true.

the IXth.

Also whethyr Ravyn came to the ship at Falmouth and ther discharged the said Walker that he shuld no further meddyll wt none of the goodes of rastell beyng in the ship and lykewyse discharged the seid Richard Mylward that he should no further meddyll wt Spicers goods and seyd it was my lord admyrall's commandment that they shuld be sold and distributed to the mareners / the said Walker sayth that Ravyn discharged hym in manner aforesaid but whether he discharged Milward or not he cannot depose.

the Xth.

Also whether Richard Walker when he came to the ship found the pakkys of Rastells fryse brokyn and the mareners havying cotes an sloppes thereof which they ware on theyr

bodys whych mareners seyd that ravyn had caused it to be delyvered by my lord admyralls comaundement the said Walker sayth that this article ys true.
the XIth.

Also whether the seyd Ravyn humfrey dyke Edward taylor and other mareners ther sold the goods of the seyd Rastel and spycer contrary to the myndes of the seyd Walker or Mylward theyr factors / that is to say salt floure fryse and other wares the said Walker sayth that the said Ravyn and others solde the goods of Rastell afor the face of the deponent and some in his absence.
the XIIth.

Also whether the seyd Ravyn wrot in his boke all that was sold and toke a rekonyng therof and reseyuyd the money and distreybutyd it as hym lyst / and whether the seyd Ravyn gaff part of the same money to the seyd Richard Mylward servant to the seyd Spicer to bryng hym home to this article the said Walker sayth he knowt not the trouthe.
13x.

Also whether Ravyn sold dyvers pipys of floure one to the prio^r of treiorow (Truro) and other mo in other places as the seyd prior and he that bought them shewyd to Richard Walker the said Walker sayth this article ys true.
14x

Also whether the seid Ravyn and other mariners spend the vitell of the seyd Rastell beying in the ship at their pleasure and went in the said ship taking the residue of the vitelles wt them to bordews contrary to the mind of the said Walker both beff, bysket, bere, bacon and other vitell by estymacion worth XXX li the said Walker cannot depose in this article for he was not present at that time.
15x

Also whethyr the seyd ravyn and other mareners caryed the residew of the goodes of the seyd rastell and spicer to bordews contrary to the myndes of the seyd Walker or Mylward /
16x

Also whythyr Ravyn delyvered at bordews certeyn of rastell's hides to one lendall servant to one maister prow to these articles he canot presisely (depose ?).

be me Rychart Walker.

Arts. 13–16 are not numbered in the M.S.

(Marginal depositions to these articles by Myrable and Bercula are here omitted.)

that he was my lordes attorney and yt he had the copy of the chartyr party and seyd it was my lords commandment that Ravyn shuld see the seyd ship occupied after Ravyns counsel and mynd to my lords most profet and seyd yt yf that Rastell wold not be orderyd by hym that he wold bryng ship and goods home agayn to my lord whyther Rastill wold or no / and incontinent therupon the seyd Ravyn in anger went down to the ship fyfe myle from Waterford / and ther the maister and Ravyn of one assent kept the ship and godes from the seyd Rastell tyl he grauntyd to follow theyr myn(des) in every thyng that they desyryd and to make aquittaunce to the seyd maister upon his obligacon and to send a letter to my lord admyrall to desyre hym to be good lord to hym to performe his viage the next yere / And that the seyd Rastell wold never have made no such quittaunce nor send the ship to bordews nor no writing to my lord admyrall but only by compulsion and for fere of losse of his goods beying then in ye seyd ship. The said Mirable sayth this article ys true. And if Restell had not condessended and agreed to the makyng of thacquitaunce at that tyme the said Ravyn was determined to have taken the said shipe and all the goodes in hyr and them to have desposed at his pleas^r.

8. It^m Wyther the seyd Ravyn brought————called Coo in to the ship of the barbara at falmouth for to go wt them and because the seyd Rastell herd sey that the seyd Coo shuld be one of the prentyse that made the insurrexcon [1] in london he warnyd Ravyn that he shuld not suffer hym to go wyth him / yet that not wtstandyng he causyd the seyd Coo to make and to pyke dyvers quarells to make debate among the souldyars / And when the seyd Rastell pacyfyed all sych quarells by good polycy and cause the seyd Coo to be put out of the barbara / yet the seyd Ravyn causyd the seyd Coo to goo into yreland in his own ship callyd the mary barkyng contrary to the mynd of the seyd Rastell and of dyvers of the souldyers the said mirable sayth this article ys true.

9. It^m Whethyr the seyd Ravyn sold and delyvered certeyn bysket of the seyd Rastells goods beying in the barbara to anothyr ship off Cornewall in the havyn of Croydon brytteyn / the said mirable knowt not the trouthe of this article.

10. It^m Wyther the seyd Ravyn and the seyd maister John Rychards provokyd oft tymys dyvers of the mariners and others

---

[1] The revolt led by apprentices against aliens in London on May Day 1517, the year of the Voyage—commonly called " the ill May-Day." It is interesting to have this picture of the agitator, Coo.

ther to make and to pyke quarelles to dyvers of the souldiers and whether one Rychard tayler one of the mariners wold have bettyn and slayn two of Rastell sevaunts at bristow y^t is to sey Thos Barkley and Thos Coke and drew his sword at them and — / the said Mirable knowt not the trouthe therof for he was not ther

per me thomas myrable

[Millward's answers are here omitted.]

Squeezed in below signature at foot of sheet.

Whyther one Rychard Smyth by the excityng of the seyd Ravyn as dyvers there thought pykyd dyvers quarells and counterfeyted dyvers lyes to make variaunce between the sowdyers and mareners / the said Myrable knowt not the trouthe.

VI. *Milward's Depositions.*

VI. *Richard Milward* of london draper of th age of XXII yeres sworn and examined saith upon his othe that the barbara tarried at Gravysende for John Ravyn howe longe this deponent know^t not but he know^t the said shipe by reason that she was felle in a leyke was broughte to grounde at plomouthe. And to the ij^{de} and iii^{de} article he know^t nothing but to the iiith / he sayth that the said Rastell made greate labor to John Rychards maister of the forsaid shipe to goo (^{to}) the see at whiche tyme Ravyn was out of the same and lackyng but how many dayes this deponent remembreth not albe the said maister aft^r retorned agayne and the other shippes went unto Ireland.

And further saith that the Vth Article is true of his owne knowledge excepte that he cannot certenly say whether the said Rastell made th acquitance for feare or saluefe garde of his goodes or not as in the said article it ys declared. And as to the VI article he saith that Ravyn had ij boyes and also made one Humfrey Dyke a gonner whereof he coulde not skyll but what wages he gave them it ys not knowe to this deponent. And saith upon hes othe that the VII Article ys true in every behalve whereof he hath perfecte knowlege, but he knowt not what answer the lorde Admirable made Walker at Blechyng (lea) ne whether he said Ravyn knewe his mynd as in the VIII article ys expressed and as deponent knowt not. Albeit Ravyn came to this deponent and discharged hym in such manner as ys declared in the IX Article. And further this deponent (saith) that Ravyn caused the marriners to have cotes of Rastells fryse saying it was my lorde Admirals (command) as in the Xth article

is truly declared. And that Ravyn and Dyke and other mariners
solde the godes of the said Rastell contrary to the mynde of
the saide Walker and this deponent in such forme as in the
XIth Article it ys declared. And that Ravyn wrote in his boke
all suche thynges as was solde and the Maister called Edward
Tailler toke and receyved the money and the said taillor and
the mariners solde all the salte and parte of the floure and the
residue John Ravyn and the mariners solde of whiche money
the said maister and Ravyn eyther of them gave the deponent
a crowne of golde. And that Ravyn and the Maryners toke
the vitalles of the said Rastell and it spede at theyr pleas[r] to
what value this deponent know[t] not.

And they carred awaye the Residue of the goods wt theym
to Rochell and burdeux contrary to the myndes of this deponent
and Walker. And that Ravyn layed upon lande at Rochell
certain hyddes of the goodes of Rastells and set a prise upon
theym.   What this deponent remembreth not ne the veary
nomber of them nevrtheles he hath them wryten in his boke.
And knowt also that Ravyn solde certain pypes of floure at
Rochell

by me Rychard Melward.

VII. *Bercula's Depositions.*

VII. Thomas Berculay of london prynter sometyme servante
unto Maister Rastell suorn and examined / (and ?) upon all and
every of th articles or intergat(at)eries brought on the behalf of
the said Rastell touchyng the viage unto the newe founde lande
at which tyme this deponent was his servante and in the said
shipe called the barbara saith and deposeth that he knowt the
same to be true excepte that he knowt not that the said Ravyn
caused wilfully a leke to be made in the said shype to th entent
to defer the viage. albeit he knowt that the shipe was caste
upon grounde whereby as it was supposed she fele in a layke.
And as to the Article touching the hyryng of the boyes or laddes
the deponent was not prive therto nor if suche secrete wordes
as was spoken between the said Rastell the maister of the shype
and the purser called John Ravyn nor knowt not of the article
tochyng the sellyng of the salte ne the Article touchyng the
wordes betwene the lorde Admirall and Rychard Walker nor
knowt not of tharticle howe Ravyn came to falmouth and
discharged the said Rychard Walker of the shype. but by
reporte nor th article tochyng the packes of fryse nor tochyng
the article of the sale of Rastelles goodes nor of the Articles

touchyng the Recepts of money nor touchyng the sale of the
floure ne of thexpendyng of the victualls ne carrage of the goods
to Bourdeux nor of the delyver of the goodes ther.   And as to
tharticle touchyng the counsaill of the maisters he knowt not
therof but he sayth that the maister of the barbara and John
Ravyn were alway famuliar and in prive counsaell togeder.
And sayth that he herde Will Hotyng say & confess all and
every article in the said Interrogatory specified of his oune word
to be true.   And further saith that he knowt his said maister
Rastell intended alway to folowe and go forward in his viage
but knowt not of thexhertacion to the contrary made by Ravyn
and the maister of the said shyppe and he confesseth that
consaill was gevyn to Rastell to fall in Robbyng wherunto he
wold never agre ne condescende ne knoweth not of th exhortacions
made at Waterford in Irland to give upe the viage ne of thex
hertacions made in Thomas Drivons house but by reporte ne of
the delivere of certain bisket bred.

per me Thomam Berculam.

RASTELL: APPENDIX II

RASTELL IN IRELAND

AMONG Rastell's many Chancery Suits is one of about the year 1534, in which he sought relief against his brother-in-law, Staverton and Dame Alice, the widow of Sir John More. The case belongs to the close of Rastell's life, when, as we have seen, he was estranged from his kinsfolk, but it carries us back to the year 1517, and shows us how he arranged for the care and maintenance of his family and servants during the three years of absence for which he made provision when he attempted his voyage to the New Found Lands.

It appears that Staverton in 1534 had taken action against Rastell for the fulfilment of outstanding obligations, and Rastell had counterclaimed against his brother-in-law and Dame Alice by submitting a reckoning that went back to the time when he " went over the seas into Yreland ". It appears that he had arranged, by prepayment, with Sir John More to keep his wife and servants for three years—apparently the time he expected to elapse before he returned from the New Found Lands. After his departure his wife, Mistress Rastell, entrusted to Staverton the sale of certain goods of her husband's lying on a quay near Billingsgate, as well as the collection of certain rents in London and Middlesex. Staverton sold the goods and for two years collected the rents, paying the money to Sir John More, who, when Rastell (after two years) " came home and requyryd the seyde money " said that what he had received from Staverton was due from Staverton himself. Rastell claimed therefore that in any reckoning between them Staverton should deduct this amount. Further, seeing that he had agreed with Sir John More for the maintenance of his family for three years, but had in fact only been absent for two, he claimed from Lady Alice and Sir John's estate £30 due to him. These family arrangements undoubtedly refer to the period of the voyage. Rastell therefore, we gather, remained in Ireland from the summer of 1517 to some time in 1519, and seeing that he deferred the prosecution of Ravyn until November 1519, this seems more than likely. He probably, therefore, wrote the play of the *Four Elements* in Ireland, and if we may judge from his reference in the play to " Ireland that holsome ground," he was not unhappy there.

He has left us a brief record of his opinion of the manners of the " wild Irish " in a passage in his *Pastyme of People* (1529). Speaking of the Danes in the time of Ethelred he writes :

> These Danys before were so proud yt they kept the husbontmen like vyleyns ; they lay in theyr housys, and ate and drank, and payed nought, and kept theyr wyfes doughters and servauntes at theyr plesurys *as the kernys and galowglashes do now in Yreland.*[1]

But if he was critical of the ways and habits of the Irish soldiery, he was alive to their readiness of wit. In his *Hundred Merry Tales* (1525) we find the following anecdote :

> One callyd Oconer an Yrish lorde toke an horseman prysoner that was one of hys gret enimys / whiche for any request or yntrety y^t ye horsman made gave iugement that he shulde incontynent be hangyd / and made a frere to shryve hym and bad hym make redy to dye. Thys frere y^t shrove hym examyned hym of dyuers synes & askyd hym among othere whyche were the gretyste synnys that ever he dyde / thys horseman answeryd & sayde . . . when I toke Oconer the laste weke in a churche and ther I myght have brennyd hym church and all . . . that same deferring of brennyng of the church . . . is one of the worst actys y^t ever I dyd wherof I moste repente . . . and I wyll never change y^t mynde what so ever shall come to my soule. This frere . . . cam to Oconer and seyd in ye name of God have some pyte uppon thys mannys sowle and let hym not dye tyll he be in a better mynde. . . . The horsman heryng ye frere thus intrete for hym sayd to Oconer thus / Oconer thou seeyst by thys mannys reporte y^t yf I dye now I am out of Charyte . . . but thou seest well y^t this frere ys a good man he is now well disposyd and in charyte / and he is redy to go to heven & so am not

[1] Spenser describes a *galloglas* as a footman, servitour or yeoman, and a *kerne* as " the proper Irish soldier ". He praises them as " very great scorners of death ", making as worthy a soldier as any nation, " but he condemns their way of life as " common ravishers of women ", men who spoil as well the subject as the enemy ".—*Present State of Ireland.*

I / therefore I pray the hang up thys frere . . . and let me
tary tyl a nother tyme y^t I may be in charyte and redy
and mete to go to hevyn. This Oconer heryng this mad
answere . . . sparyd the man and forgave hym hys lyfe at
that season.

On 25th October, 1519, after his return from Ireland, Rastell
printed a work that may have occupied him during his absence.
The *Abbreviation of the Statutes* is to be distinguished from
Fitzherbert's *Abridgment of Cases*. It is a small Law Dictionary,
whose peculiar distinction is that it is the first of its kind to be
published in English. *Abridgments of the Statutes* had been
printed by Pynson, Machlinia and others before 1500 in their
original Law-French. It fell to Rastell to be the first to
translate an Abridgment into English and publish it for the use
of Law students. The significance of his enterprise is not to
be underestimated. Translation was one of the most potent
instruments of the New Learning as well as of the Reformation.
The Latin Grammars of Colet, Lily and Linacre written in
English were, like the New Testament of Erasmus, revolutionary.
They disturbed a tradition of pedantry and clericalism. Professional obscurity, whether in law, medicine, theology or
education, is not to be dissipated, however, except at the risk
of condemnation for unprofessional conduct or even heresy.
And just as the writer on golf warns his reader that all his
instructions as to grip and stance count as nothing where a
course of lessons is possible from his Club professional, so Rastell
advises those of his readers who are in doubt to consult " some
man that ys lernyd in the laws ".

Rastell's naïve and intimate preface, which in due course his
son William piously republished, may be read in Herbert's
Ames. It traces the history of Law-French, mentions the
reforms of Edward III, who ordained that actions should be
pleaded in English, and records how " the second Salomon ",
Henry VII, recognizing the amendment and growth of the vulgar
tongue, decreed that the Statutes should henceforth be "endited,
written, published and printed in English ".

As in the earlier prefaces, we must particularly notice that
Rastell protests that he is working for the commonweal, and if
it be suggested that he " protesteth too much " we may point
out that his prefaces are never addressed to a patron. " No
person," says Latimer, " is born into the World for his own
sake, but for the Commonweal's sake." The teaching of the
Latimers and Rastells may have had no small share in the

development of the sense of statesmanship and patriotism that
marked Elizabethan-days.

The colophon of the *Abbreviacion* is of interest as showing
that Rastell procured from the King a grant of monopoly
protecting his work for seven years :

> Thus endyth the abbreviac̃on of statutes, translated out
> of French into English by John Rastell and Imprinted by
> the same John the XXV day of October in the XI yere
> of the reign of our sovereyn lord kyng Henry the VIII,
> with the pryvylege of our seyd soverein lord grauntyd to
> the seyd John, that no nother imprint agayn thys seid
> work nor no nother ellis where printyd of them sell wythin
> thys realme duryng the space of VII yeres next after this
> furst impression.

When the seven years had elapsed Rastell republished the
work (1527) and possibly claimed a renewal of his monopoly
in virtue thereof, despite the limitation implied in the phrase
" after this first impression ". If so, he failed ; for Robert
Redman issued in 1528 an edition differing little from Rastell's.
Redman's relations with Rastell, however, are somewhat mys-
terious. I am of opinion that Rastell had an understanding
with Redman.

LAW BOOKS AND PREFACES (1513-19)

THE three great Law Books that Rastell printed before he moved to Paul's Gate call for special notice. They were the *Liber Assisarum* (1513), the *Grand Abridgment* (1516), and the *Table of the Grand Abridgment* (12th February, 1518-19).

From the time of Edward I up to 1535, when they came to an end, there had been flowing the great stream of law reports or *Year Books*. These were arranged by terms, the Hilary Term (beginning 23rd or 24th January), the Easter Term (beginning seventeen days after Easter Day), the Trinity Term (beginning on the Wednesday after Corpus Christi day), and the Michaelmas Term (beginning on the 9th or 10th October). It is to these Terms and to his collection of *Year Books* that Chaucer refers when he says of his Serjeant of Law :

> In *termes* hadde he caas and doomes alle
> That fro the tyme of kyng William were falle.

In the *Grand Abridgment*, by Anthony Fitzherbert, for some time Recorder of Coventry, we have a concise summary of the *Year Books*, to which it formed a useful index, just as they are themselves the best index to the Pleas enrolled. There are three important *Abridgments*—by Nicholas Statham, printed by Tailleur of Rouen about 1490; by Fitzherbert, printed by Rastell (1516); and by Sir Robert Broke, printed by Tottel (1568). The Law Reports of Edward III were subjected to a second and independent summarization in the *Boke of the Assises*. These are more concise than the *Year Books*, giving rather the gist of the argument and the decision than a report of proceedings, but they are fuller than the *Abridgments*.

The *Liber Assisarum* was Rastell's first big book. Though undated, it undoubtedly belongs to the year 1513. His son William so dates it in his re-issue, printed by Tottel in 1561, when he repeated the "Prologus Johannis Rastel in laudam legum, Anno V Henricus VIII ". John Rastell had himself indicated the date on page 5 of his edition in the list he gives of the judges on circuit :

> Here folow the names of the sherys in englande and the names of the Justices of every cyrcute in the fyft yere (i.e. 1513) of the rayne of our soverein lord kyng henry the VIII.

In the dated edition (1561) of William Rastell's *Le Liver des Assises* we find similarly recorded :

> Here folow the names of the sheres . . . in the third yere of the raign of our souerain Lady Elizabeth.

And whilst among the judges in the earlier list we find Sir John More, we find in the latter Wilhelmus Rastell unus Justic. dñe regine. In each case the list of judges is correct for the year of publication.

The substance of John Rastell's first preface, piously and very properly reproduced, as we have seen, in 1561 by his son, may be abbreviated as follows :

Throughout the nations of the civilized world nothing is held more worthy than the commonweal, and he is most praised and honourably renowned who most endeavours to augment it. Yet poets, orators, philosophers and learned men have failed to agree as to what constitutes this commonweal. Some say that it consists in abundant riches, some in power and strength, some in honour and glory, others, like the Romans, in a combination of riches, power and glory. To Rastell, whatever it is, it " must needs of itself be a good thing, where unto some goodness naturally is annexed " ; for God, " the fountain of all goodness ", has implanted in man a universal love and zeal towards it.

Being therefore in itself a good thing, the furtherance of the commonweal cannot involve the doing of any evil to others. Now the pursuit of wealth involves the poverty of others, great puissance in one nation implies relative weakness in another, and great glory a corresponding shame and reproof. Wealth, power and glory are therefore in themselves evil things, since they cannot be achieved except at the cost of impoverishment, subjection and humiliation. They cannot, for that reason, constitute the commonweal.

" Now under correction," he continues, " after myne opinion

The Bishop of Winchester replied: " Mr. Rastell what ye meane by the law of nature, of man and of God, I can not tell, but of this I am sure that the vilest partes in the creature of nature takes most labours and paynes / and contrary the chefest members whiche are set next to the noble bloud labour least. And as concernyng the law of man, etc. . . .

" To whiche reasons Mr. Rastell made no answer, but song agayne his old song / of which the Archbishop of Canterburie was werye and said if he had any new reasons they shuld be heard / but as for the old they be sufficiently knowen ".— (Record Office, *Theological Tracts*, IX. 19.)

"THE PASTYME OF PEOPLE"

DURING the year 1529 Rastell was engaged on the compilation of his well-known chronicle, *The Pastyme of People*. Like Fabyan, whose Chronicle, printed by Pynson in 1516, he follows closely, he closes with the reign of Richard III, and he contributes therefore nothing directly to our knowledge of his own time. Yet the fidelity with which he borrows the phraseology of his predecessor has its value, for it enables us at once to indicate his own contributions or asides. These give to the *Pastyme* an independent value, and merit special consideration. Equally independent are the bold woodcuts of the kings of England from William I to Richard III. Rastell may have taken the idea of these from the portraits of the kings of England in the fifteenth-century window of St. Mary's Hall, Coventry, whilst the boldness of the lines, the general disposition of the designs and the accompaniment of armorial shields suggest that his illustrations may also have been designed originally for a series of figures in stained glass.

It is proposed to gather here some of the more striking of the comments and critical additions that give to the *Pastyme* its value as an index to the mind of its compiler.

In the Prologue he traverses the legendary origin of the name of Albion and Geoffrey of Monmouth's story of Brute, of whom he points out that Gildas and Bede have nothing to say. It was Caesar, he insists, who first described Britain, and this claim for a more critical appreciation of Caesar's *Commentaries* gains interest, as we have seen, from the fact that William Rastell in 1530, shortly after the Prologue was written, printed the first English text and translation of the chapters referring to Britain.

The same critical attitude is found in the account of Bladud, the legendary founder of Bath, " a grete nigromancer who by that craft made there the hote Bathys"; but philosophers hold, he adds, that as there are in Italy and elsewhere hot fumes and smokings perpetually rising from the earth, so when any "well spring brekyth out . . . when such a hote fume is nigh joyning . . . then it will naturally make the water hote ".

Like Polydore Vergil, he writes sceptically and at length of Geoffrey of Monmouth's account of Arthur, pointing out that Bede, who wrote of the British kings before and after him, does not mention him. Indeed, " some suppose that Galfryde wrote that story for affection, because he was a Welchman borne in the tyme of King Henry the II ". He adds that there was hanging on the shrine of St. Edward at Westminster a seal bearing the legend, "Arthurus patricius Brittaniae Gallie et Dacie Imperator", taken from a supposed deed granted by Arthur to the Abbey, but this too would seem " to be a thynge fayned of late by some man havyng affeccion to Arthur ", for the Abbey was founded after Arthur's time on " a wyld busshy place . . . callyd Thorney ". He doubts the existence of pre-Conquest seals of wax. He is sceptical too of Geoffrey's story of the death of Ursula and her maidens at Cologne, and he refers to his blunders in dealing with Ina, King of Wessex.

Rastell's criticisms show his lines of interest or his own experience when he likens the Danes to the Kernys and Galowglashies of his own day in Ireland, or when he decides that if William II built Westminster Hall, it must have been an earlier building, seeing that in the stone and timber work the arms are those of Richard II, the three lions and the fleurs-de-lis quarterly with the badge of the white hart. The foundations, he says, may be possibly Rufus' work or that part of the White Hall "above the steyres ". In any case no king of England bore the arms of France before Edward III ; and on points of heraldry Rastell is sound, as the shields on his royal portraits show. Similarly we may cite under Aurelius Ambrose the disquisition on the nature of the stones at Stonehenge. His comment too on the beginning of printing at Mayence is characteristic : " which craft is nowe mervaylously increasyd . . . and have been the cause of many thynges and great chaunges, and is lyke to be the cause of many straunge thynges here after to come."

In his reference to the foundation of the Order of the Garter by Edward III, he says that some hold that the founder was Richard I, who honoured twenty-six knights who had fought grimly at Acre by conferring upon them the distinction of

Cwyllyam Conquerour.

FROM 'THE PASTYME OF PEOPLE'   FROM THE FIFTEENTH-CENTURY WINDOW
                                      IN ST. MARY'S HALL, COVENTRY

WILLIAM THE CONQUEROR

wearing thongs of blue leather about their legs, whence they were called " Knyghtes of the blewe thong ".

In John's reign, Fabyan does not mention Magna Carta, but Rastell not only tells of the meeting near Staines at " Runney Mede ", but emphasizes the confirmation of the charter in the eighth year of Henry III, and the addition then of certain articles touching wardship and marriage. He was professionally interested in legal history, and writes in praise of the " Westminster primer " with its " goodly statutes ", of felonious clerks, of assise, of pleas of land and attaints. He is full of praise for the wisdom of Edward III and the many good statutes his twenty-five Parliaments added to the books. He established the laws " mervelously well ". The same legal interest is seen in his note on the dating of records after the restoration of Henry VI, when he tells us " all wrytynges and recordes were made and dated thus : ' Anno ab instauratione regni regis Henrici Sexti quadragesimo nono, et anno readoptionis sui regii magestatis primo ' ".

He was much interested in measures and money values. Speaking of a dearth in the reign of Edward I, when corn sold at forty shillings a quarter, he explains the price by pointing out that then an ounce of silver made twenty pence ; whereas Henry VI lowered the value of money by coining thirty pence from the ounce, Edward IV forty pence, whilst in his own day Henry VIII had made the ounce run to three shillings and eight pence. Yet the weight of an ounce troy had " remained ever at one stynt, namely that thirty-two greynes of whete drye and rounde, and takyn in the middes of ye ere shuld wey a sterlynge peny ; and twenty of those sterlynge pens shulde make an unce and twelve unce shulde make a pounde troy; and VIII pounds troy shuld wey a galon of wyne ; and VIII galons of wine shulde make a busshel of London, which is the VIII parte of a quarter ". In speaking of the depreciation of the current coin, he carefully distinguishes, therefore, the penny sterling (or twentieth part of the ounce) from the forty-four parts of an ounce, " callyd IIIs and VIIId." When Edward III established his coinage of gold and silver, he ordained that the twenty pence sterling should make a farthing of gold, twelve of which farthings should weigh an ounce.

It was Rastell's interest in money values that led him to disclose the date of his writing. In the section dealing with the reign of Henry IV we read that Richard II left treasure to the value of seven thousand pounds. " But yet here," he

adds "ye must note that X/s in these dayes was better than
X/s is at this present day, whyche is nowe the XXI yere of our
souerayn kynge Henry VIII (1529), for at those dayes V grotes
made an ounce and nowe at this day XI grotes maketh an
ounce." (Grote = four pence sterling.) He shows the same
interest in measures. The standard foot was determined, he
says, under Henry III ; "III barley corns, drye and rounde
shulde make an ynche and XII ynches to a fote, and III fote
to a yarde and V yardes and a halfe to a perche or pole, and
XL pole in lengthe and four in brede, to make an acre of lande ",
which standards of weight and length, he tells us, were confirmed
by Edward III, Henry VI, Edward IV, and in the XI year of
Henry VII.

It is not surprising, in view of the interest he betrays in
measures, that Rastell acted on a Commission in 1533 granting
acquittance to the Goldsmiths, who minted at the Tower for
the legitimacy of their minting from March to October, "the
money having been found good ".

There are certain interesting minor departures from Fabyan
that show that Rastell made independent use of the earlier
authorities. Thus among the thirty-two kings whose names
alone appear in Fabyan as ruling after Elidorus, Rastell distinguishes Bledgabredus the twenty-third by adding : "He
excelled all other in connyng of musyk, and in pleying uppon
all maner of instrumentys of musyk, that the people callyd hym
the god of melody ". What though Bledgabredus be but the
shadow of a shade, he seems to say, there have been and are
gods of melody.

In the same way he honours Gerbonianus, son of Morwyd,
"who byldyd Camebryge and Grauntam, and was welbelovyd
of his people " because "he maynteynd poore laborers and
husbandmen, and wold suffer no lord nor other to do them
wrong ".

And this leads us to one of Rastell's most characteristic
asides. It should be noticed first, however, that the *Pastyme*
contains a summary of Roman history omitted by Fabyan.
Under the article "Publius Valerius Publicola", he notes with
approval that Roman Dictators were held responsible at the
end of their term of office for all acts of injustice, and
"answerable to all byllis and complayntis" alleged against
them. Hence, he says, arose the "indyffrent justyce" of the
Romans, as well as their greatness and high renown. "Wold
God it were so usyd at this day in England, that every jugge

or other offycers havynge auctoryte to execute ye lawis or to gouerne or to rule in any office should be remouable at IIII or V yere or lesse, and then to answere to all complayntes that shuld be allegid agayns him . . . and then ther wold not be so mich extorcione and oppressione of the pore people, nor so many iniuries as is now a days ". He returns to this point in speaking of Edward I and the Inquisition of Trolbaston, when a searching inquiry was made into the misdemeanours of mayors, sheriffs, bailiffs, escheators and others whereby the king's coffers were filled. " Nevertheless," adds Rastell, " the kynge did greate good . . . for those offenders were . . . moche more meeker and better, and the pore commons lyved in moche more rest and peace."

Another notable departure from Fabyan is found in his attention to the tortures and dreadful deaths of Edward II, Humphrey, Duke of Gloucester, and of the two princes. The account of the opinions held in Rastell's day of the pitiful tragedy of the young princes has a peculiar interest as being the only contemporary event recorded in the *Pastyme* on which Rastell speaks with independence.

Despite the fact that the *Pastyme* makes no claim to be more than a brief compilation or outline, we have shown that it has a peculiar value as the work of a known writer of independent views. He had the critical instinct that goes to the making of a historian; he was a man of liberal views with a keen sense of the claims of the " poor commons ", but perhaps his deeper convictions were nowhere more simply or sincerely expressed than in the Roman section under Augustus, where we read :

In the xlii year of his empyre, Jhesu Chryste, the son of God, and second person in Trinite, took mannes nature, and was borne in the cyte of Bedlem in Jury, of the Virgyn Mary, concyvyd without mannes seed, by the inspiracyon of the Holy Gost, as apperith in the bokes of the IIII Evangelistis, Mark, Mathew, Luke and John, which wrote of his godhead, manhood, workes and myracles. He taught and prechyd a new law, exorting all men to meeknes and charite, rebuking syn and despising war ; all contrary to the mindes of the gret kinges and gouernours of the Romans and sich other ; but he dyspisyd all worldly honour, conquest and victory, and taught and exortid everi man to love his enemy, and to do good for yuyll.

concernyng theyr own besynes / yet for a recreacyon amonge
them self / they be desyrous eche of other to know news and
straunge thynges of other contrees.   And as it happenyd to me
on a season to be in companye of dyvers of these marchauntys /
amonge them all specyall there were II of them / of the whyche
one was a turke called Gyngemyn borne under Machometys law /
and ye other was a Christenman callyd Comyngo / borne in hye
Almayn / whyche were of olde famylyer accoyntaunce / and
bothe of them men of great wytte and of good lernynge / and
specyally ye turk / whyche was well lernyd bothe in morall
phylosophye and naturall / betwene whom I herde mych good
communycacion / argumentys and reasons / whych lyked me very
well / and so wel pleased me that immedyately after that I toke
penne and ynk and tytled it in wrytynge / and reported every
argument and reason as nygh as my wytte and remembraunce
wold serue me / after the maner as here after foloweth in this
lytell boke.   And in the begynnynge of theyr sayd communy-
cacyon Comyngo the Almayn asked of Gyngemyn the Turke
what tythynges or newes were in his contrey / whych Gyngemyn
shewed hym of the great warres whych ye great Turke had
lately had in dyvers places / as well as of the great sege of ye
Rodes / as of the great batayles / whych he had lately had in
hungarye.   But yet the sayde Gyngemyn was not so glad to
tel the tythynges and news in and about his contrey / as he
was desyrous to knowe of some straunge news in other places
in Christendom.   And oft tymes required this Comyngo to shew
hym some new tythynges of his contrey.   To ye whych Comyngo
the Almayne answered and shewed hym that there was a newe
varyaunce in Christendome and a scysme begonne of late amonge
the people there / concernynge theyr fayth and beleve / and sayd
that there was a new opinyon spronge among the people / that
there is no purgatory / nor that the soule of man after it is
separate from the body / shal never be purged nor puryfyed of
no synne that remayneth therin / but yt it shal immedyatly
after it is separate from the body / go to heven to eternall ioy
and salvacyon / or ellys to hell to eternall payne and damp-
nacyon.   To whom Gyngemyn answered and sayd that ye
opynyon was but folysh and agayns all good naturall reason /
by cause that all people in ye world of what contrey so ever
they have been or be / or of what law and secte so ever they
have been or be / as wel the Panyms / the Jewes / and you that
be of Chrysten fayth / and we that be of Machomets law / and
all other that ever lyved or do lyve after the order of any good

reason / have ever byleved and do byleve that there is a purgatory / where mannes soules shall be purged after this mortall lyfe. Therfore quod he I mervell greatly that there shuld any such fond opynyon begynne amonge the people now in any contrey / consyderynge yt there is no reason to maynteyne theyr opynyon that ever I coude here. To whom Comyngo ye Almayne answered and sayd that they had dyvers reasons to maynteyne theyr opinion there.

(Here follow in seven statements Comyngo's exposition of " the reasons of them that holde opinyon that there is no purgatory ").

To whom this Gyngemyn the turke anone answered and sayd / that as for all these reasons they me be sone answered and avoyded / and yf thou wylt gyve to me dylygent heryng / I shall gyve the suffycyent solucions to al those reasons and satisfye thy mynde. And further I shal prove to thee by other argumentes and by natural reason and good phylosophye / yt there must nedys be a purgatory / where ye soule of man after yt is separat from the body / shalbe purged and puryfyed. To whom then Comyngo sayde / yt he wold be mervelous glad to here his mynde therin. To whom this Gyngemyn then sayd / yt he must immedyatly go in to the strete to speke with a marchaunt / to aske of hym but one short question touchyng ye besynes of his marchaundyse / and sayd that he wold retorne agayne incontynent / which as he sayd / he dyd / and taryed not long but shortly cam agayn. And as sone as ever they were mete there agayn / they began theyr communycacion / and Comyngo ye Almayn began fyrst to speke / and sayd as hereafter now foloweth.

Finis prologi.

hede that he neyther smyte to shorte of the lyne nor yet under / for then it is a losse and he had better let it go. And fynallye sometyme a man smyteth over and thynketh al wonne / and yet an ungracious poste stondeth in the way and maketh the ball to rebounde backe agayne over the corde and loseth the game. And that wyl anger a man / and I assartayne yow that ye have tossed never a ball but ye offend in one of these poyntes / and yet besydes that somtyme ye play a touche of legerdemayne and caste me a ball which when it commythe I perceaue to be none of myne / and all the courte shall iudge the same."

Rastell had apparently alleged that Frith aimed at amusing " chyldren foles and madmen " by raising laughter. It is as though he were to expound *In principio erat Verbum*

In the begynnyng of this yere
John Frith is a noble clerke &c.

To this Frith replies : " If I wold saye theyr were no wytte in Rastell's hede / then wolde he conclude that theyr were no wytte in no mannes hede / he hath so longe studied phylosophye / that he hath cleare forgotten his principals of sophistry / not-wythstanding we wyll forgive him the faut for the man is somwhat aged and therfore I thynke it is long syns he reade them / and that they are now oute of his memory."

He then turns to the verses : " For the rime and meter they myght wel say that a gose had made it for any reason that is therin / and as touchyng the meter / the seconde verse lacketh a fote & is shorter than his fellowes / but if you putte out this worde Frith and put in this word Rastell for it / then shall his meter also be perfeyte / and that haltinge verse shall runne merelye wyth his felowes uppon his ryght feet on this manr

In the begynnyng of this yere
John Rastell was a noble clerk . . .

" Thus have I amended his meter / but as for the reason I leve it to himselfe to amende it at his leysure." Frith concludes on an interesting personal note. " I am in continual feare bothe of the Levetenant and of my keper lest they shulde espye any bokes by me ; and therfore it is lyttel mervel though the worke be onperfryt, for whensoever I here the keyes ringe at the dore / strayte al muste be conueyed out of the waye /

and then yf any notable thinges hadd been in my minde / it is
clene lost."

More resigned the Chancellorship in May 1532 and therefore
had no association with the imprisonment and examination of
Frith, who was sent to the Tower early in 1533 and to the stake
on 3rd July.

oratione meditata longaque et quae binis ferme concionibus
essent satis, oblatrabat in coena. Summa rationum tota
pendebat e miraculis, quorum nobis effutiebat e *Mariali*
multa : tum quaedam ex aliis ejusdem farinae libellis, quos
afferri jubet in mensam, quo narrationi major accedat
auctoritas. Quum aliquando tandem perorasset, ego
modeste respondi, primum nihil esse toto illo sermone dictum, quo res persuadeatur illis, si qui forte quae recensuerat
miracula non admitterent, quod fors accidere salva Christi
fide possit ; quae tamensi ut maxime vera sint, ad rem
haudquaquam satis habere momenti. Nam ut facile reperias
principem, qui condonet interdum vel hostibus aliquid ad
preces matris : ita nullus est usquam tam stultus, qui
promulget legem qua suorum audaciam in semet provocat
impunitate promissa proditoribus, quicumque genetricem
ejus certo demereatur obsequio. Multis ultro citroque
dictis, effeci tandem ut ille tolleretur laudibus, ipse pro
stulto riderer.

TRANSLATION.

Lambeth. Codex Wharton 595.

(in the hand of Wm. Sancroft Archbp 1678–1691)

Sylloge epistolarum quarundem insignium . . . facta manu
R.R.P. Wilhelmi Sancroft Archiēpi Cantuar etc.

No. 4.

(An old printed book entitled Epistolae aliquot erudatorum
nunquam antehac excusae. They are eight in all and ye last
Sir Tho. Mores to a monk unnam'd; left out in his English works
and in his Latin both at Basel in 8° 1563 and at Louvain in
fol. 1566 on purpose sure because it made agst them. But Mr.
Day y^t wrote ye Descant on Davids Psalmes borrowed it of
Mr. Henry Jackson fellow of C.C.C. in Oxford & hath inserted
ye translation of p̄t of it in preface to ye Reader. . . . Sancroft's
description of contents of Sylloge)

There was (seth Sir Th. More in y^t Epistle) at Coventry a
Fryar of ye number of those Franciscans wch were not as yet
reformed to ye Rule of St Francis. This man preached in y^e
Citie, in ye suburbs, in ye towns & villages thereabout y^t
Quicunque Psalterium B. Virginin oraret quotidie nunq posse
damnari.[1] This was no sooner delivered, but it was so easily

[1] Whosoever said daily Our Lady's Psalter never could be damned.

heard & as readily believed for ye shewd so easy a way to Heaven. The pastor of ye place, an honest & learned man, though for his own part he knew well enough y^t it was but foolishly spoken yet dissembled a while supposing that no harm would ensue thereupon; & y^t ye people the more addicted they were to the worship of ye Blessed Virgin, ye more religious they would be. At ubi tandem recognoscens ovile deprehendit ea scabie vehementer infectum gregem; pessimum quemque in illo psalterio max religiosum esse [1] upon no other mind and purpose than to dare to do anything so that there was no doubt at all but they should have Heaven wch so grave an Author as ye Fryar, fallen from Heaven, unto them so faithfully promised: then at length he began to admonish his people y^t they sh^d not trust too much to ye saying of ye psalter, tho say it they should no less y^n ten times a Day: yt certainly they did well who said it well over, so they said it not over upon y^t confidence wherewith all others had now begun. Otherwise y^t much better it was to omitt those prayers altogether, so they would omitt those crimes too wch under ye patronage of these prayers they did so confidently commit. This when once he had spoken to them out of ye pulpit, twas strange how waspish they were. They challenge him for his word; they hiss at him; they drive him out of y^r company and defame him as an enemy to ye Virgin Mary. The Fryer another day up to ye pulpit with all speed; & to vex Mr. Parson the more begins with this theme; Dignare me laudare te Virgo sacrata; Da mihi virtutem contra hostes tuos.[2] For they say a certain Scot did use the self same Theme, being to dispute at Paris of ye Virgins Immaculate Conception; qui Lutetiam in momento delatum periclitante scilicet alioque beata Virgine millia passuum plusquam trecenta mentiuntur.[3] But what need (so) many words; the short and the long was this; ye Fryar easily persuaded those y^t were willing enough to believe that their pastor was a fool yea and a wicked man too.

Now while all this was in this hurly burly it so fell out y^t my self had occasion to go to Coventry, to see a sister of mine

---

[1] But when in due time he inspected his sheepfold he found that his flock were stricken with rot, and that the worst were those that were most strict in their use of the Psalter.

[2] Grant me to magnify Thee, Holy Virgin, strengthen me against thine enemies.

[3] And they add the lie that Paris in a moment was borne away three hundred miles and more, for in good sooth the Blessed Virgin had otherwise been in some peril.

RASTELL'S HOUSE AND STAGE IN FINSBURY FIELDS

BETWEEN Old Street and the north wall of the City lay the playing fields of the apprentices. Originally a piece of marshy ground known as Moorfields and Finsbury Fields, it had been reclaimed by an elaborate system of sewers or ditches and causeys, and was much resorted to for archery, wrestling and games. All that remains of the old archery ground now is the space occupied by the parade ground of the Honourable Artillery Company between City Road and Bunhill Row ; whilst adjoining it on the north the burying-ground of Bunhill Fields preserves for other purposes a little more of the old playground. In this burying-ground lie the bodies of Bunyan, Defoe, Isaac Watts, Susannah Wesley and William Blake. Elsewhere this ancient suburb of the City has been heavily overbuilt.

Hall and Stowe speak of the encroachment upon these open spaces by private persons who enclosed gardens with hedges and ditches for their own pleasure, so that the apprentices were constrained to retaliate by levelling and filling them. " Nevertheless," Stowe adds, " now we see the thing in worse case than ever, by means of enclosures for gardens, wherein are builded many fayr summer houses . . . some of them like Midsummer Pageants with Towers, Turrets and Chimney Tops, not so much for use or profit as for shewe and pleasure."

The western boundary of this open ground was Whitecross Street, which runs from St. Giles, Cripplegate, northward to Old Street ; but between Whitecross Street and Bunhill Row, which runs parallel to it on the east, was a belt of encroachments which in Rastell's day was too far gone to admit of public dispute. At the north end of this belt he leased at Michaelmas 1524 a piece of open ground of one and three-quarter acres on which he built himself a house and erected his stage. Although he would, we are told, reside for months at a time at his other house at Hadley, " he used most commonly to lye in his house by Fynnesbury Felds ".

As this district became important later in the history of the Elizabethan stage, it may be well to show the evidence we have for determining the position of " Rastell's grounds ".

" On the Feast of Saint Michael in the sixteenth year of Henry VIII " an indenture, now filed with the Conventual Leases (Middlesex 33) at the Record Office, was made between Dame Joan Lynde, Prioress of Holywell, and " John Rastell of London, Gentylman ", leasing to him for the term of forty-one years, 1 acre 3 roods of ground lying in the Lordship or Manor of Finsbury. It extended in length from the Priory lands in Finsbury Fields on the east to the land of Henry Frowyk on the west, and in depth from Old Street on the north to the farm of Finsbury on the south. The annual rent was twenty shillings, and Rastell undertook to build a house or houses, of the value of 20 marks or more, which on the expiry of the lease should become the property of the Priory. As Rastell's death in 1536 was followed almost immediately by the dissolution of the monasteries, we are able to follow the history of the property.

It was bounded on the west, as we have seen, by the land of Henry Frowyk [1] which we learn from his will (18 Porch) was known as the Manor of Gloucesters, and this manor was bounded on the west by Whitecross Street. On the north side of Rastell's ground ran the highway, on the south the farm or manor of Finsbury. Of this manor, which belonged to a prebend of St. Paul's, there is material for an interesting piece of research in the *Book of Records for the Manner of Fynnesbury* (1551–1830),[2] the transactions of the Court Baron.

It appears from these Manor records that Rastell's successor, one Roger Medcalf, in 1565 " stopped the comen sewer " or drain against his house in Old Street, and choked the ditch between his ground and Gloucesters with weeds and rubbish. Thereafter the Medcalfs appeared repeatedly as offenders against the customs of the manor, until in 1592 they showed the court their lease, and how they held not of the manor but of the Crown, as the successors of John Rastell, a tenant of Holywell Priory. The position of Rastell's property is thus indicated by frequent references in the Manor records, and, aided by Henry Ellis's *History of Shoreditch* and by Stowe, we find that

---

[1] The memory of Frowyk, who was a neighbour of Rastell's near Hadley is preserved by the Frowyk Chantry in South Mimms church.

[2] Guildhall MS. 96.

JOHN HEYWOOD, THE DRAMATIST: CONFUSION WITH OTHERS OF THE SAME NAME

CONTEMPORARY with the dramatist were several Heywoods named John, whom it is well to keep distinct. There was an innkeeper of Henley-on-Thames, a steward and agent of Sir Adrian Fortescue. As Fortescue was executed for treason in 1539 his papers are among the State Papers at the Record Office, and the Henley innkeeper by this circumstance troubles the dramatist's biographers.

Secondly there was a Minor Canon of St. Paul's, named John Hayward, but misnamed Heywood by Strype—or his compositor—in his *Life of Grindal*, an error which led Mr. Grattan Flood and others to inferences as to the dramatist's connection with St. Paul's. The Minor Canon signed, as John Hayward, the *Acknowledgements of the King's Supremacy* along with the other members of the cathedral establishment in 1534, but to make the point secure I obtained permission to transcribe the report in the Bishop of London's records of Grindal's visitation of St. Paul's in 1562, and found that Strype was wrong. Other Heywoods have been rashly identified with the dramatist, particularly among the tenants whose names have come into the State Papers in the mass of particulars contained in monastic leases and gathered by the King's Surveyors of Lands at the dissolution of the monasteries.

A more important confusion, however, is that with a John Heywood who was already in the royal service as a yeoman of the Crown when the dramatist entered the Court service as a singer in 1519. Collier supports his statement that Heywood was connected with the household in 1514 by the following extract from the King's Book of Payments [1]:

6 Henry VIII. Jan. 6. To John Haywood wages 8^d per day.

This reference, however, is entirely misleading. Collier

[1] Dr. Wallace only copies Collier's extract, and, like him, misdates it.

abstracted one name from an entry containing the names of twenty-four yeomen of the Crown. The item ought to have been given as follows :

21st January, Anno VI. *Item* paid to Thomas Jayes, John Holland, John Con, Richard Rider, Robert Griffiths, William Whiteacres, George Hodgekynson, Thomas Creme, Edward Ecka, James Mason, John ap Richards, Piers Motton, Thomas Vaughan, and John Alen, every of them at XIId the day. And to *John Haywoode*, William Vaughan, Morice Matthews, Morice Comport, Christopher Tolly, Jenkin Davy, Walter Jagowe, Thomas Cooke, and John Mason at VIIId the day, and Roger Salesbury at VId the day for their months wages of December last past whiche the kinges grace hathe given them.

That the twenty-four were yeomen of the Crown there can be no doubt. Jayes, Holland, Con, Rider, Griffiths, Whiteacres, Creme, Ecka, James Mason and Tolly all drew their livery of russet and black on 18th December, 1514, according to the Cofferer's accounts (Excheq. a/cs. 418/5). Alen was drawing his livery in 1509, Hodgekynson (27/3/12), Richards (21/3/16), Motton (May 1520), Wm. Vaughan (1509–14), Jagowe (14/12/17) and John Mason (21/3/16) appear in the Letters and Papers of Henry VIII as yeomen of the Crown under the dates given. Thomas Vaughan is described as Serjeant-at-Arms in the Auditors' Patent Book I, page 78. Comport appears as yeoman in the Egerton fragment of 1525, and a John Heywood was pensioned as a groom of the household in the same year (a/cs. 419/13), whilst in 1520 in the Accounts of the Duke of Buckingham there occurs the item, " to oon John Haiwode oon of the yomen of the Crowne bringing tithings unto the said duc . . . from therle of Surrey out of Ireland, 6/8 ".

The household accounts show the payment of the guard regularly month by month without names under the formula[1]: " for the wages of 170 yeomen of the Chamber as well of XIId by the day, and VIIId by the day, as also of VId by the day, as by a roll of their names subscribed by Sir Henry Marney Kt., Captain of the King's Guard, doth appear for the present month of June, which yeomen he discharged of their daily attendance upon the king in this present month ". The entry of 21st January, 1514/5, is preceded by such an item, and the fact that the payment we are considering was an extraordinary one, " which

---

[1] I select the entry for June 1515 as typical.

and the arrerages thereof to helpe me now in my old yeares for my fynding & Relieffe here in these parties being weake & unable to traveill & passe the Seas at this my extreame age. Whereof I trust her Majestie by the good furtherance of your honor & my good Ladie will have a pittifull consideration. Thus I beseche god to blesse and save your good honor & my ever good Ladie & all yours ffrome Mechlyne this 4 of Septembre 1575

your humbyll
JHON HEYWOOD.

Addressed. To the right honorable my singular good Lord, the Lorde Burghley Lord heighe Treasuror off England.

[Cecil Papers 8/44.]

It is worth while in reading this very pleasing letter playfully to emphasize—as I am sure Heywood meant it—the eight references to " my good Ladie " and to note particularly the " my good Ladie *as aforesaid* ". In his earlier letter he lamented that his hearing was beginning to fail him and his mirth " decaying with age ". Something of his mirth remained to the end.

MEDWALL: APPENDIX

PRIOR GOLDSTONE'S SUIT AGAINST HENRY MEDWALL

(Early Chancery Proceedings, 238–2. Date of Suit, 2nd to 9th February, 1500–1)

To the reverent fader in God the Bisshop of Salisbury [1] and Chauncellor of Engelond.

MEKELY besechith your good lordship your contynuel oratour Thomas Priour [2] of the Chirche of Criste of Caunterbury Ordynarie of all the spirituell Jurisdicion in the provynce of Caunterbury by reason of the Cee of Caunterbury nowe beyng voide by the disseas of the most reverent fader in God John late Cardynall and Archiepisshop of Caunterbury.[3] that whereas the seid Priour and all other his predecessours Priours of the seid Chirche in the right of the same Chirche by all the tyme out of mynde have hadde ymmediatly after the disseas of every Archiepisshop of Caunterbury the seid Cee so beyng voide all ordinarie and spirituele Iurisdiccon withyn the provynce. And that the seid Priour and all his predecessours priours of the seid Chirche by all the seid tyme have used to make depute and ordeigne all Commissaries officialls Registres scribes fermours and all other officers and mynysters concernyng the seid spirituell Iurisdiccon : by reason wherof all bokes registers evedences recordes escrites and mynymentes concernyng the seid spirituell Iurisdiccon as well beyng in the kepyng of all Commissaries and officialls as in the kepyng of all Registers scribes or other officers or Ministers whatsoever they be concernyng or belongyng to the seid Ordinarie and spirituel Iurisdiccon of right belong and perteyne

---

[1] Henry Deane, who succeeded Morton as Chancellor on 23rd October, 1500.

[2] Thomas Goldstone II, Prior, 1494–1517.

[3] John Morton, d. 22nd October, 1500.

And ought to belong and apperteyne to the seid Priour duryng the tyme of vacacion of the seid Cee of Caunterbury / So it is that meny and dyvers bokes registers evidences recordes estretes and minymentes concernyng and belongyng to the seid Ordinarie and spirituell Iurisdiccon byne come to the handes and possession of one henry Medewall / and oftentymes sithens the disseas of the seid lord Cardynall your seid oratour hath required the seid henry to delyvere unto hym all the seid bokes registers evidences recordes estretes and mynymentes : which to do the seid henry hath alwey refused and yet doith refuse. For as moch as the nomber and certaynte of all the seid bokes registers evidences and recordes estretes and mynyments be to your seid oratour unknowen And they be not in eny chiste lokked bagge or boxe ensealid your seid oratour is without remedy by the course of the comen lawe / Wherfore that it may please your good lordship, the premisses tenderly considered to graunt a Writ of subpena to be directed to the seid henry commaundyng hym by the same to appere before the kyng in his Chauncery at a certayn day and under a certayn peyn by your lordship to be lymited he there to do answer and receyve on the premisses as therappon shall be considered accordyng to ryght and good conscience. And this for the love of God And in the wey of charite

Edūs lichefelde de London
Gentelman

Humfrius Gay de eadem
Gentelman

Endorsed Coram domino Rege in Cancellaria sua in Octavis Purificionis beate Marie proxime futuris (i.e. 2–9 February, 1500–1).

INDEX

A and B, see *Fulgens and Lucres*
Abbreviation of the Statutes, 20, 177, 204
Ad imprimendum solum, 181 ff.
Albright, Miss E. M., 186 *n*.
Alleyne, Edward, 232
Amicitia, De, 77
Andrewe, Lawrence, 17, 174
Andrewe, Mistress, bookseller, 17, 174 (2)
Arabic numbers, 208, 209
— Arnold, bookseller, 174
Arundel, John, 23
Astronomy, 18–20

Baker, David Erskine, 122
Baldwin, William, 65–6
Bale, John, 179
Bang, Professor, 70
Banks, Richard, bookseller, 174, 184
Barbara, the, 11, 188 ff.
Barclay, Alexander, 13
Barnes, Friar, 169
Barnet, Battle of, 1
Bartlett, Thomas, *see* also Berthelet, Bercula, 174
Belknap, Sir Edward, 7, 8, 15
Bercula(y), Thomas, printer, 12, 172, 188
Berthelet, Thomas, printer, 169 ff., 172, 184
Beware the Cat, 65
Bible in English, 3, 6
Birch, George, actor, 232
Blackwall, 189 ff.
Boas, F. S., 96, 100, 103
Bonaccorso of Pistoja, 97
Bonam, William, bookseller, 174
Bonde, Thomas, of Coventry, 3, 4
Book of the Charge, The, 24
Booksellers of London, 165 ff.

Book trade, regulation of, 160 ff.
Braintree, 56 *n*.
Bridge House case, 12
Butsbery, 31–2, 35
Byddell, John, printer, 178
Byrd, Roger, 4

Cabot, Sebastian, 12, 187
Caesar's *Commentaries*, 76–7, 211
Calais, 6
Calisto and Meliboea, 17, 94, 112–16
Canones Astrologici, 20
Capel, Bromwich, 4
Caxton, William, 97 ff., 177
Cecil, William, Lord Burleigh, 35–7, 237–8
Chambers, Sir Edmund, 233
Chancery Bills, frivolous, 20
Charterhouse, 2, 25
Chelmsford, 56 *n*.
Child-bishop, 4
Cholmeley, Sir Roger, 33
Cicero, 77, 98
Clement, Dr. John, 47–8, 67–8, 71, 87–8, 92, 155–6
Clement, Margaret, 88, 153, 156
Coke, Thomas, 188 ff.
Colet, John, 163
Collier, J. Payne, 95 ff., 100
Collyns, John, bookseller, 174
Comfort against Tribulation, 84, 89
Coo, an agitator, 189 ff.
Cooke, Sir Anthony, 37
Cooke, Mildred (" My good Ladie "), wife of Lord Burleigh, 35–7, 237–8
Cooke, Richard, 3, 6
Copland, Robert, bookseller, 174
Copyright, 176 ff.
Corley, 4
Cornyshe, William, 38, 95, 144, 145

R

241

PRINTED IN GREAT BRITAIN
BY UNWIN BROTHERS, LIMITED
LONDON AND WOKING